The Rearing of an American Evangelical

The Rearing of an American Evangelical

Jeff Hood

WIPF & STOCK · Eugene, Oregon

THE REARING OF AN AMERICAN EVANGELICAL

Copyright © 2016 Jeff Hood. All rights reserved. Except for brief quotations in critical publications or reviews, no part of this book may be reproduced in any manner without prior written permission from the publisher. Write: Permissions, Wipf and Stock Publishers, 199 W. 8th Ave., Suite 3, Eugene, OR 97401.

Wipf & Stock
An Imprint of Wipf and Stock Publishers
199 W. 8th Ave., Suite 3
Eugene, OR 97401

www.wipfandstock.com

PAPERBACK ISBN: 978-1-5326-1250-3
HARDCOVER ISBN: 978-1-5326-1252-7

Manufactured in the U.S.A.   NOVEMBER 29, 2016

For Madeleine & Lucas

"God always makes a way out of no way." The pastors shouted the words over and over. Throughout my childhood, we believed in a very narrow way. I never found God there. I was always haunted by something else. Told through both fact and fiction, this is the story of how.

Beginnings

God was always there. I guess.

    I grew up in a loving household. My parents were young and followed convictions handed down to them by their parents. The earliest convictions that found me were their earliest convictions. Love, fights fueled by alcohol, selfishness, homemade costumes, compassion and a plethora of other things consistently reminded us of our humanity and made us dream of more. We made it.

    I was raised to be a particular type of Christian. We are a species that trap and cage our deficiencies behind glowing smiles. I never understood such ways of being. My parents are not perfect...but love is love. This is a story of love.

    I remember God. The divine was a construct used to guide and discipline my brother and I. God was never on our side. When I was three, I got spanked for the first time. The slaps across my backside were particularly painful and I was told they were also a means of grace. From this moment forward, every time I received a spanking, I was told, "God loves you and so do I...this is why I must spank you." If these words were meant to educate me that love came from a blunt hand slapping my ass, then they did the trick. From this moment on I knew God as a stinging, confusing and painful kind of love.

Dad is selfless. We played it all. In the car, Dad inxxztroduced us to Will Smith, Jazzy Jeff, MC Hammer and Vanilla Ice. I remember riding with Dad and rapping (ok maybe it was more like singing) at the tops of our lungs, "Vanilla Ice-Ice-Baby…too cold…too cold…" Dad's career as a firefighter and paramedic brought us much pride. Every night we got the chance, we headed over to the fire station and Dad filled the night sky with an array of powerful sirens and lights. Those were brilliant days. We didn't know about the tragedies.

Decapitations, burned corpses, brutal car accidents, moaning victims, screaming families, spewing blood and missing limbs were standard encounters for Dad. We had no idea of the damage that was being done to his mental health…neither did he. Every night when Dad closed his eyes, the terror would return. I remember the soft cries and sleepless nights.

Grandaddy demanded much more than my parents were capable of. On his days off, Dad worked at Grandaddy's business. Though the money was good, Dad was treated like shit. In the midst of it all, Dad turned to alcohol. The weekends were all the same. Friday and Saturday was filled with drunken debauchery. Sunday was for church. Dad was young and having to grow too fast. I knew the pain of expectations early.

I can remember being forced to pray over my most egregious sins. When I stole candy from the store, I had to pray. When I flashed my penis at passing cars, I had to pray. When I had a sip of my father's beer, I had to pray. I began to understand prayer as punishment. God had a heavy hand and an angry personality. I was only four.

Mom is tough. In the midst of youthful ignorance, Mom loved and provided for us as best she could. I can never remember an occasion that Mom didn't go all out. On my third birthday, Mom had a guy dressed up as Big Bird come to my daycare. I don't think I have ever been more frightened of anything. I cried. Mom created an acrobatic troop called the Bambinies. She pushed our entire bodies up on her feet and we would feel like we were flying. I soared. Mom weaned me off a bottle by letting me throw it out the window. I grieved. Mom threw us into the pool over and over again. I swam. The lessons were often tough. The love was always relentless.

The wounds were always festering. Hurt people hurt people. Dad drank too much. Unable to maintain control, Mom grew abusive as well. The fights were monumental. Objects and insults flew through the air. I remember the violent tears. Teenagers shouldn't get married. Twenty is too young to get pregnant. The odds were stacked against her. With no other outlets, Mom turned her rage toward us. Toys, belts, electrical chords and a variety of other weapons regularly met my body. Blood flowed on a variety of occasions. I didn't know then what I do now. I come from a long line of sufferers of mental illness.

    Mom grew up in an abusive home. Things got worse when she married Dad. Unable to see the value of their marriage, my grandparents pressured Mom to leave Dad. Told she was fat, lazy and unsuccessful, Mom was subject to constant verbal abuse. We were pawns in the game. After loaning my parents money to buy their first house, my grandparents threatened to call the loan over and over again. One particularly painful moment arrived in the form of a Lego set.

    Christmas is usually a joyful time for most kids. I remember it always being complicated for us. Mom saved her money for months to buy me a Lego set. Excited to build it with me, Mom beamed. After sneaking the set to the car the next day, my grandparents went to the toy store and exchanged the present for some video games. I came home and Mom cried. She kept asking God for help. I knew God wasn't listening. The pain only intensified.

I learned a strange prayer growing up, "Now I lay me down to sleep, I pray the Lord my soul to keep, If I die before I wake, I pray the Lord my soul to take." I remember many nights laying down, closing my eyes and experiencing visions of violent death. The prayer was hopeless. As a young child, I was afraid to die. God seemed like the biggest terrorist of them all.

Though a few years younger, my brother accompanied me through the terrors. He used to cry his eyeballs out and beg my parents not to get divorced. I think my brother's tears kept them together. His humor and rebellion made me dream about something more. I remember my brother often looking into my young fundamentalist eyes and saying, "You dare me to cus?" Somewhat scared and somewhat excited I said, "Yes!!!" My brother let it rip, "shit, ass, damn, and hell..." Though I told Mom each time, I always admired his courage. In the difficult hours, my pain was his pain and his pain was my pain. I guess God knew I needed a companion through all of this crazy shit.

In the midst of my earliest dreams and nightmares, God hated me and I him. To set the tone, I had to tell you about it. I am the product of a peculiar group of people. I am an American Evangelical and this is my rearing.

Church

The house of the God is often a house of horror.

When I was five-years-old, I sat in a semi-circle with about fifteen other children in a class led by Mrs. Sally. We could see that there were three posters lying facedown on the table next to her. She was a nice woman with a soft wrinkled face, sweet smile and relaxed demeanor...at least until she got going with these stories. Us kids knew the routine and waited expectantly for the reading of the first of two verses. We were told that the story would unfold in three parts. Mrs. Sally began glowingly, "Mark 10 Verse 14, Permit the children to come to Me; do not hinder them; for the Kingdom of God belongs to such as these." She held up the first illustration poster. Jesus was sitting on a rock surrounded by fifty children of a variety of colors. One part of the illustration stood out...there was one little boy who did not join the rest of the children and stood awkwardly to the side. Mrs. Sally pointed out the solitary boy and then told us that Jesus wants all of the children to come and play with him.

Paying the solitary boy no mind, I imagined giving Jesus a high five. I loved him...until we got to the second part of the story. Mrs. Sally's expression quickly changed as she read the second verse, "Mark 10 Verse 15, Truly I say to you, whoever does not receive the kingdom of God like a little child will not enter it at all." After reading the passage, she reminded us of the little boy that was off to the side in the previous illustration. I forgot about him and remained transfixed on Jesus. Mrs. Sally, eager to bring things home for us little kids, changed her smiling expression into a scowl and whipped up the second illustration.

    The picture was of the little boy standing at the gates of heaven knocking on the door and there was no one there to let him in. We knew he was at heaven, because we could see the sign hanging above the doors. Particularly noticeable in this illustration, was a red glow that was ruminating from the bottom corner, in tremendous contrast to the rest of the glowing tones of yellow and white. Mrs. Sally told us that the little boy was not getting to go to heaven because he did not play with Jesus while he was on earth. Knowing from previous talks that heaven was the place you want to be, all of us kids got tremendously scarred and wondered if we had played with Jesus enough here on earth. Before we had time to completely think about all of these truths and consequences, Mrs. Sally angrily held up the last poster illustration of the little boy engulfed in flames and being prodded with a pitchfork by what we knew to be the devil, which looked like something from a horror film. She exclaimed, "If only he had played with Jesus when he was asked to...he would not of found himself burning in HELL!"

Some kids started crying and when some of the helpers tried to console the kids...Mrs. Sally motioned for them to stay with her right hand. I had a wide-eyed expression on my face and was terrified. Mrs. Sally then explained to us the way that we could play with Jesus and make sure we got to heaven was by saying the prayer for sinners. She began, "Lord Jesus, I know that I am a sinner, I repent of my sins, I ask you to come into my heart, and I want to live in heaven with you forever." Mrs. Sally asked who had accepted Jesus that day and everyone in the room raised their hands. When she left the room, Mrs. Sally seemed to feel better and slickly remarked to a co-helper, "I knew we would get them all saved today with that lesson." Strangely, although I accepted the story and prayer that she gave, I didn't feel much better for it. Though Mrs. Sally passed away a few years ago, I can still see and hear her voice often in my nightmares. In my youngest years, my church taught me to be incredibly afraid of Jesus...needless to say, this is not where I first experienced God's love.

The big brown leather chair that sat outside Mrs. Violet's office was reserved for the worst of kids. Those who acted up got sent out of their classroom and had to sit in that hallway leather chair until their parents angrily and embarrassingly arrived to pick them up. Teacher's jokingly called it the "judgment chair" and gleefully remarked that the chair was "for the little demons...somewhere close to the gates of Hell." For much of my childhood, I found myself sitting there, in that big brown leather chair, for my egregious deeds. Many of my teachers didn't know what to do with me.

I was a wild child. I consistently acted up when I was supposed to be serious. I couldn't understand why my teachers were telling me about this Jesus who wanted to celebrate with me and consistently made me sit down, shut-up and eat my cookies and juice. I wanted to move around and enjoy the fellowship. This was not to be. When my teachers talked about sin, somehow the big brown leather chair always came up. All of us kids knew that God didn't love the child in that chair. While I sat there, I often felt alone, unloved and ostracized. This pattern continued for a number of years, until one day a little brown boy named Ralph, that a member of the church had adopted, showed up for class.

From the moment I met him, I liked Ralph, but I could tell no one else in my class did. I played with Ralph, while all the rest of the kids and teachers stayed on the other side of the room, pointing and laughing. I noticed that Ralph consistently got in trouble with the teachers for not doing anything. One of the common stories was that he was touching and kissing the little girls. Ralph took my place in the big brown leather chair. At first, I thought it was great. I thought that I'd been saved from further parental love spankings and feelings of God's abandonment. After a while, I began to wonder what was going on with Ralph. One little girl named Joan remarked, "My mommy told me not to go near that trashy boy." The other kids laughed and giggled while pointing at Ralph. I overheard the teacher, Mrs. Cynthia, remark, "No matter how hard you try, you just can't control trash." I saw Ralph cry a few times as I looked out the door. Ultimately, I garnered the courage to ask Mrs. Cynthia why Ralph kept on getting sent out of the room for doing nothing. She angrily replied, "Are you going to cast your lot with trash?" Not knowing what she meant, I walked away. The other kids knew that I was fond of Ralph and made fun of me for it. It was in this environment that I realized that the God I was learning about didn't care too much for the outcast.

      Going to the gym with my dad was always a treat for my brother and I. While my dad played basketball with the adults, we were free to rip and romp throughout the church. We absolutely loved it. I am convinced that some of the fiercest competitions I will ever experienced occurred on one of those small red, white and blue basketball goals for kids. One night as my dad played on the big goal and we played on the small goal, an older homeless gentleman came into the gym and asked the group of about twelve leaders of our church if he could have some money for food. The interrogation came quickly and stunningly. As my father stood back with another young man, the older men demanded, "Where do you live?" "What do you want this money for?" "Is this for drugs and booze?" "Are you drunk right now?" "Where are you going after this?" "How are you going to get more money?" The questions were relentless. The entire situation reminded me of a story I had been read by my parents a few days prior. The Children's Storybook of the Bible was a constant presence at our house and the previous week we had read the story of Jesus' arrest and prosecution. The voices of the older men sounded very similar to the shrill voices that I had imagined a few nights prior flowing from the Pharisees. As I was thinking about the story, I realized that the homeless man was beginning to cry as he talked about his family and their many needs. As I watched, I felt shivers running down my spine and tears beginning to well up in my eyes. I felt so miserable and crummy for the way that the man was being treated. The older men, however, would simply not let up with the questions, accusations and condemnations. Ultimately, after about thirty minutes, the older men tossed twenty dollars at the man and told him to beat it. They turned around and talked amongst themselves as if they had accomplished something. I can even remember one older man returning and remarking, "That's how the church needs to handle these beggars." I felt that the only thing that they had accomplished or handled was managing to completely demean the man who needed their help. It was at this point that I realized that God didn't like poor people either.

    These stories speak of my earliest memories I had of the concept of God. HE was angry, hateful and picked oppressed people. No matter how often I try to destruct and reeducate myself, these images seem to arise occasionally in the nether regions of my mind. I imagine the boy being tormented and destroyed by Satan, Ralph sitting in the big brown leather chair and the poor gentleman begging for money and fearfully struggle with a question: Is that the real God? I hope not. Faith is the assurance of things hoped for.

Grandparents

Always respect your elders?

In January of 1987, my world was rocked. For a few months, I prayed for the arrival of my brother. It all sounded great at the time. I guess it didn't register to me that another human being was about to join our family. I enjoyed being the center of attention. I was consistently told how smart, cute and funny I was. I loved it. When I was told that I was going to stay at my grandparents for a few days while mommy went to get the baby, I still didn't get it. Then, my grandmother woke me early one morning to tell me that God had blessed me with a new little brother. We rushed to the hospital.

I can remember thinking that it didn't feel like a blessing to be running around in the middle of the night. We arrived at the hospital and I refused to get out of the car. I was a spoiled brat. My grandmother kept speaking of God's love, grace and patience to coax me out of the car. Finally, my grandfather had enough and jerked me out. Not realizing her excitement, my grandmother slammed the door before he could get me out. After exclaiming, "My Lord!" as if she were at a high-powered worship service, I was rushed to the emergency room. The result was four stitches and a pseudo-religious unquestionably mystical lighting-bolt white scar on my forehead. God's new blessing really hurt.

From the commotion around the baby, I realized I shared the spotlight of youthful bliss with another. After a short round of treatment, I was ushered by my parents to see the red powdery bundle of flesh and goo. I ended up getting to hold my brother that night and realized that life was no longer just about me. At the age of three, this is an unbelievably huge lesson. My grandmother's consistent moans of "Thank you Jesus!" helped further educate me that, good, bad, or ugly, Jesus was responsible for all of this.

If my paternal grandparents were simple people, my maternal grandparents were unquestionably not. My grandfather ran away from an impoverished home at age 13, got a girl pregnant at 18, married and divorced by 21, married my grandmother and had my mom by 32 and was a millionaire owner of a small business by the age of 40. My grandmother didn't have much of anything growing up, spent her career working for Delta and enjoyed the wealth she shared with her husband as much as anything. Though I knew from a very early age that both sets of my grandparents were racist, my maternal grandfather was the most vocal and cantankerous about it. Perhaps a product of being raised in a backwoods Appalachian world where he was made fun of for being the grandson of a Union sympathizer during the Civil War, granddaddy was never able to let his fears of and anger at black people go.

I went to a small Christian preschool for three years. For my parents, this was a means by which to educate me in the evangelical faith. For my grandparents, this was a way to keep me away from the black children at the public school who might somehow contaminate me. When my grandparents offered to pay for it, the dye was cast and the deal was done. I began preschool and learned that every letter in English has a corresponding word and picture from the Bible. Through daily recitation of the Pledge of Allegiance, singing of the National Anthem, prayers for the troops, recitation of the Pledge to the Bible, discussion of the value of being an American and recitation of the Pledge to the Christian Flag- which had strangely similar colors to the U.S. flag- I learned what it meant to be a good Christian.

The United States was not just the center of our world...it was also the center of our Christian faith. Though it might sound strange, I can honestly say that it was pounded into my head by association and alliteration that Jesus was a white southerner. Both sets of my exceedingly patriotic grandparents loved it. During this time, I was taught that men were to be the protectors of women. By opening doors and treating women gently, I was playing my role. By the time I was five, I had been completely educated as to the ins and outs of the entirety of Southern whiteness, citizenry and masculinity. It was as if my preschool was a southern evangelical finishing school. I guess in many ways it was. Desperate to fulfill the roles laid out before me, I went to work.

    I recited the pledges really loud, prayed extra hard, played extra hard with my G.I. Joes, read my Children's Storybook Bible, championed the United States in every way I could imagine, tried to become smart so that I too could serve the country and dreamed of marrying a beautiful woman and having lots of money to help my faith and country. The teachers loved seeing this in me and remarked glowingly to my parents of my consistent progress. In the minds of the surrounding evangelical community, I was already at the top of my game. For such progress, I was chosen for a high honor...reciting the Christmas Story at our Christmas pageant. My assignment was to memorize Luke 2:1-20. My parents and grandparents were thrilled. My mom worked hard to help me memorize the passage and after a few weeks I had it. When the night came, I dressed in traditional southern attire, a blue suit and yellow beau-tie. I was very excited. I knew that the moment had arrived to prove how smart and evangelical I was. I stood and delivered. The audience was shocked that all of those words came from my memory as I stood speaking. I delivered a rousing rendition of Jesus' birth. The audience cheered and my family cried. I credit my mom with helping me memorize all of those lines. Unfortunately, I thought Jesus was a white southern American and probably was born somewhere around Birmingham. I guess I figured that the writers of the Bible just misspelled Bethlehem. My grandparents might not have ever been prouder. They told everyone about it. For my grandparents, I was well on my way to a happy, prosperous and meaningful life. The next big fight was just around the corner…as my family considered whether or not to send me to public school the next year.

Sunday dinners were an incredibly educational time for me. My entire family would gather at the home of my grandparents for food and gossip. I found out everything that was going on at church and in the community over the standard weekly fair of pot roast, cream corn, green beans, mashed potatoes and apple pies. My grandfather spoke of his business and when things were down it was always the fault of the blacks. My grandmother discussed the girls at the beauty shop and summarized her numerous weekly rendezvous while shopping at the local mall. My dad talked about the horrors of the past week. My mom wanted to go back to school and talked expectantly about it with my grandparents in hopes that they might pick up the tab. My brother and I would just sit quietly and occasionally get in trouble for flicking pieces of corn at each other. We were never really a part of the conversation.

Before the big blow-up, the only time I can remember being talked about in previous animated conversation was when I peed next to my grandfather before dinner and remarked how big I thought his penis was. My grandfather loved it and glowingly remarked to everyone at dinner that I thought his penis was enormous. Looking back, I guess his bragging was rather strange and peculiar, but back then I just felt embarrassed and kept on eating. Later that spring, the blow-up arrived. As the pork roast was being sliced one Sunday, my mom made an intentionally subdued remark, "I think we are going to enroll Jeffrey at the local public school." My grandfather responded with full force, "What the Hell Did YOU Just Say!?!? If you want him to be the only white boy sitting in a room full of niggers, then go right ahead, but don't expect me to be supportive or fund this little social experiment. Besides, I thought ya'll wanted him to go to school with Jesus and religion…" I was very proud of my mother that day. She stood her ground, telling them that she believed in public education and thought that public schools offered much more space for intellectual growth than private schools could. It was one of the first times I had seen her stand up to my wealthy and often overbearing grandfather.

    Throughout the conversation, I pushed my pork roast around on my plate and thought about what was said. I had a ton of respect and love for my grandfather, he was the main tree house constructor and master fisherman in my life, and I reflected deeply on what he said. I suspected that the public school would be full of little black children waiting hungrily and expectantly for one little white child. I had never had any black friends and suspected from the way my grandfather talked that the black children would eat a little white boy like me alive. I worried about my grandfather's use of the word experiment, as I had earlier in the week watched a television program that showed mice being experimented on with electric impulses. I could just imagine myself sitting in a classroom with little electric conductors placed all over my body. What is 1+1? 3? Shock. Learning by electric shock therapy didn't sound like too much fun. I was excited with the thought of not having to go to school with Jesus anymore. I got enough of him in my church's fear and damnation classes on Sundays and Wednesdays. Regardless of all my fears and excitements, I trusted my mother's direction for my life. I knew she wouldn't steer me wrong. So when I was asked at dinner where I wanted to go to school, I replied, "the public school please." My grandfather immediately responded, "Oh shit."

When I first walked into the school, I wondered if my grandfather was right. There were a bunch of black kids and they looked at me suspiciously. As I walked into Mrs. Bellington's classroom, I took a big chance and sat down to play with four black boys, two black girls, two Hispanic boys and an Asian girl. At first, I thought it strange that the ten white kids were playing together at the other end of the classroom. Then after some thought, I figured that they had grandfathers similar to mine. Unfortunately, the classroom did seem like an experimental laboratory and I felt like there were people standing over us writing things down at all times. After two weeks, my teacher came to me and said that, due to overcrowding, I was no longer going to be in her class. I was surprised and hurt by this news. I had genuinely come to enjoy and appreciate most of the kids in my class. Like a prisoner being led to trial to await their eternal fate, I solemnly and bravely walked down the hall to the classroom. When Mrs. Ellington greeted me, I couldn't take my eyes off her warm smile. After sitting down to my desk, I looked around to realize that all the kids were scared too. Mrs. Ellington's kindness to everyone and my accumulation of many new friends made the situation transform from tolerable to great. Then I went home.

"You aren't seriously thinking about letting him stay in that nigger teacher's class?" The question rolled around in my head over and over. Despite his fierce anger, my mother refused to budge. I hadn't realized that Mrs. Ellington was black. After listening to more conversation and arguing, I realized that Mrs. Ellington was the first black teacher at my elementary school. I didn't care what my grandfather said...I loved her.

The room darkened and the film came on. The story was of a bright rambunctious young Christian boy who grew up to become an amazing man. The ending gripped me like nothing else had ever before, "I have a dream my four little children will one day live in a nation where they will not be judged by the color of their skin but by the content of their character...Let freedom ring! Let freedom ring! Let freedom ring!...*until that day when* we will all be able to speed up the day when...all of God's children...will be able to join hands and *sing*, 'Free at last, free at last; thank God Almighty, we are free at last.'" When the light came on, out of pure joy and excitement, I jumped up and down and waived my hands in the air as I had seen people do on a gospel television show. Mrs. Ellington asked me to calm down. To reward my enthusiasm, she assigned me the task of memorizing the last few paragraphs of Dr. Martin Luther King, Jr.'s infamous "I Have a Dream" speech. As mentioned earlier, I was good at memorization. Again with my mom's help, I memorized and recited the speech with gusto in front of a large group of students. During this time, Mrs. Ellington was also actively teaching us about Dr. King and his legacy. For those two weeks, I could not wait to get to school and was moved daily.

    At the end of the second week, my grandparents picked me up from school to spend the night. We went to Red Lobster, their absolute favorite restaurant, and had a tremendous time. My grandfather always made the day's dinner, usually a lobster, verbally commune with us and I found it to be like going to some type of seafood show. I loved going there and sometimes still do. Later that night, I was riding in my grandparent's Cadillac Seville and my grandmother asked a pertinent question, "What have you been learning about at school?" I thought they would never ask and excitedly told them, "I have been learning about Dr. Martin Luther King, Jr., his 'I Have a Dream' speech, his ways of Christian non-violence and his current residence in heaven." Close to the house, my grandfather snapped back, "What the fuck did you just say?" As we inched up the driveway at the house, he continued, "If all they are going to teach the boy is about the niggers and coons then we have to get him out of the public school system! This is a nightmare! They are ruining the boy at five! I knew this was an absolutely fucking terrible idea." I had never heard this word 'fuck' before, but I knew from the tone of his voice that it was not a nice word and probably one I shouldn't repeat. After my grandmother calmed my grandfather down, I spent the night at their house, as I often did. The next morning, I could hear my grandfather screaming through the phone receiver and calling my mom dumb and ignorant for sending me to public school. I remember my grandfather poignantly remarking, "We are going to lose him."

  War raged in the Persian Gulf. I was amazed at all of the military action on television. Between footage of the conflict, I remember my parents reminding us that we must pray for and support the troops fighting for our Christian values. In the midst of all of this, I wondered who was praying for the other troops and families being hurt and killed? If my parents were patriotic, my grandparents took things to a whole new level. My grandfather served in the South Pacific during and after World War II. One afternoon, as I sat at my grandparents' house, I got the nerve to ask my grandmother about the other people dying in Iraq and she swiftly replied, "They don't matter. Don't you know the story of Israel?" I remembered the story of Moses leading the nation of Israel out of Egypt and all of the Egyptians who were killed in the process. I responded in the affirmative. "They were God's chosen people and the lineage continues. Now, America is God's chosen nation. Get it?" I didn't know where she was going with these comments and I prodded, "But Jesus wasn't an American?" "If Jesus was alive today he would be an American, I'm convinced of that," she snapped back, "Your granddaddy was fighting for his faith when his served in the army...don't you dare disrespect that!" Knowing that there were at the very least Christian missionaries overseas, I prodded one more time, "But what about the Christians over there?" She got angrier and popped back, "Don't you know that only Southern Baptists and United Methodists are going to heaven?" At the time, this didn't sound too bad, as the only Christians I knew were Southern Baptists and United Methodists. After the contentious conversation, my grandmother reverted back to her usual musings of faith. "I can't wait to climb that golden ladder to go see Jesus." I knew that seeing Jesus meant death. The whole prospect of death and dying scared me. My grandmother didn't stop, "We have got to work extra hard here on earth so that God will give us enough strength to step up on each golden heavenly rung after we are dead. You know every time you are bad here you lose a rung in your ladder that you are going to need later?" I was imagining this miles long golden ladder stretching into the sky all the way to heaven and trying to be good enough on earth to get all the rungs I needed to get to the top. The task seemed scary, daunting and impossible. Thankfully, the phone rang and interrupted the conversation. "Hey Betty, how are you?" she rambled on and on until asking the final question, "Are you going to come by and pick up my recycling to drop off at the nigger church?" Not long after that, my parents arrived to pick me up, I was glad. I had enough. Faith at my grandmother's house was always a strange and frightening mix of nationalism, morbidity and racism.

I knew about the divine importance of money from a very early age. My grandfather created a carbonation company and made it big. Somewhere between a runaway at 13 and a millionaire at 40, my grandfather met his gods. They were usually green and had pictures of presidents on them. At some point in his career, my grandfather also decided that Republicans protected his gods the best. There were two things that I remember my grandfather watching with gusto, the stock market and elections. My grandfather often reminded me, "The market and those damned elections determine whether we live like kings or paupers son." I admired my grandfather- he was the expert builder of tree houses- and I knew that I wanted to live like a king, so I became a Republican too.

Somewhere between second and third grade, I got incredibly interested in presidential politics. These were exciting times. I remember Ross Perot, George Bush and Bill Clinton fighting it out in the 1992 presidential race. The homes of one side of grandparents were Bush Country. I overheard my grandfather and knew that I was supposed to think that "Clinton was a sexual predator and would take away all of our money." So I was shocked, a few days later, when I heard my other grandmother remark, "Clinton is a good Baptist and wants to help poor people like Roosevelt did." I didn't listen. I followed what my granddaddy said, "The only reason that people are poor is because they don't want to work. Clinton just wants to help people not work. That's why they love him." Sometime around October, I began to second-guess my previous assumptions. I had long realized that a girl in my group was poor. She often wore tattered clothes and received free lunch. Based on my grandfather's advice, I figured her parents were just sorry white people and didn't want to work. I was not very nice to her. I thought she stunk. "She was not one of our people," I thought. One day to be extra mean, I broke a new pencil that she bought at the school store. My teacher saw me break the pencil and immediately took me out of the class. She demanded to know why I broke the pencil. "Because she is poor!" I daringly replied. My teacher began to cry, "She is poor because her parents died, she was being punched in the face by her grandfather and now lives at the Rainbow Foster Home." I felt lower than whale shit. I began to cry and remembered something my mom read to me about Jesus loving poor people. I knew that I was in the wrong. I went in and apologized to the girl. I bought her five new pencils and we became quick friends. I first learned about grace from the poor girl in my class.

Most of the time, my grandmother was everything a grandson could ask for. She let us spend the night at their house all the time and spoiled us. We got to eat cheerios, fruit snacks, popsicles, drink orange juice and watch movies until we fell over asleep or got sick. Grandmother picked us up from school often and, against my mother's consistent exhortations, took us to get fries almost daily. Thanks to my grandfather's earnings, we got just about anything we wanted. My first pair of Jordans came in the third grade. I still remember them, black, multi-colored, wraps in the front, and the Michael Jordan peace logo at the top. It was not all about money, grandmother was a generally fun person to be around. She was willing to take risks with us, including riding in a wagon down steep embankments, wading in the nasty creek behind their house and going on safaris with us deep into the woods at their lake house. Grandmother desperately wanted to spend all the time she could with us. Ours was a world of gluttony and we loved every minute of it. Needless to say, we spent a ton of time with my grandmother.

Because they knew that they were unable, my parents allowed my grandparents to spend this kind of money on us. This did not cause problems until my parents began to loose control. When my grandparents went overboard, my parents begged them to stop. They wouldn't. There were also moments were I felt the sting of inequality directed at me at my cousin. He got far less time and attention than we did. On Christmas, my grandparents would hold two separate Christmases, one for just our family and the other for everyone. It was always a big secret that we were doing the other celebration. We would secretly get a ton more stuff than my cousin ever did the night before Christmas and then get even more the next day. We went to Disney World multiple times, as a family, without my cousin or his family. My parents allowed this activity to go on and by omission approved it. It took some time before us kids we realized what was going. Throughout my childhood, my grandmother spoiled us, but there was also a dark side to the gifts and affections. Such revelations, however, would come later.

After World War II, I guess things were no longer quite as exciting for my grandfather as they had been. Everyday, after a beer or two out at the barn, my grandfather would come in for lunch. Although mom and the preacher told me that alcohol was the devil, my grandfather's drinking didn't bother me too much. I guess in comparison to my dad it seemed tame. Immediately after lunch, in the midst of my grandmother's incessant talking, my grandfather would rush to go sit in his big recliner, hurriedly flip on the television, and watch *As The World Turns* as if he were a zombie. At church, our preacher used to talk about *As The World Turns* and other trashy television shows, once remarking "Those who watch such filth as soap operas and sitcoms are not worthy of the Kingdom of Heaven!" Every time he said something damning like that, I always thought it was really funny that my grandfather was a prominent deacon at the church, a semi-closeted drinker and the most avid soap opera watcher I have ever known. It might sound strange, but I learned to ignore some of the cultural rhetoric coming out of our preacher's mouth due to my grandfather's witness and dedication to his beers and his soap operas. For this unintended lesson, I will always be grateful.

Dreams

What are you learning?

    We were all about education. Our family drilled it into me daily. From a young age, my mother pushed me. Books were our means of fun. I can remember my mom and dad reading Dr. Seuss books and the Children's Bible Storybook over and over again. I am convinced that anything that I accomplish as an intellectual in life is a direct result of the time my parents spent with those silly books and me. Each year, I got to pick a character from one of the books and my mom would sew me the costume for Halloween. It was a smashing good time. She once created a Batman suit for me that I wore for about a year afterwards. My dad was more of a sports and adventure guy. He taught us how to play sorts of sports. We thought my dad was the guy who could beat Bo Jackson at anything...the second greatest all-around athlete in the world for those who were unaware. We were fans of the Georgia Bulldogs and the Atlanta Falcons, Braves, and Hawks, probably in that order. When Atlantan Boxer Evander Holyfield won the Heavyweight Championship of the World, we all celebrated in our underwear. After hearing that Atlanta got chosen for the 1996 Olympiad on the radio, we danced and praised God with hands raised in the bedroom with my mother. When Sid slid to beat the Pittsburgh Pirates and the Atlanta Braves won the 1991 National League Championship, we celebrated mightily with the rest of the city. Creativity, intellectual fervor and sports all played large roles in my formulations of God. I knew from a very early age that anything claiming to be God had to be creative, smart and athletic. I had a series of dreams when I was a child where God was in my class at school. God was the brilliant artistic athletic kid that everyone looked up to. God was my friend and loved everyone equally. During my earliest years, I am convinced that God was challenging the assumptions I got from the church through those dreams. There were also nightmares.

    I have always had a clear sense of evil. The man in the top hat is why. To think about him, even today, sends shivers down my spine. For much of my early life, I consistently dreamed that a huge slumped mole-filled gnarly-looking green man in a top hat carrying a cane was coming through my bedroom door to get me every night. He never spoke and walked directly to my bed to stand over me. For years, I was terrified and woke up discussing his features. By the end of first grade, however, the man in the top hat began to speak. He called me worthless, sorry, disgusting, filthy and a host of other things. When people ask me if I believe in the devil or demons, I point back to the green man in the top hat. I don't think it is any coincidence that my parents were struggling in their marriage about this same time. My dad was drinking too much with the boys and my mom was very angry at life in general. For most of her life, my mother had been given everything she could have ever wanted, but by her late twenties she felt that she had accomplished very little. There were alcohol-fueled fights and moments of utter rage. My mom would throw things at my dad and he would leave. My mom would demand that my father stay home, hide his keys and the next thing I knew he was riding down the street on his lawnmower. Talk of divorce was consistent. My brother and I would cry, begging them to stop. We were young and they were too. My grandfather offered my mom a house and car if she would leave my dad. The confluence of events pushed life to the breaking point. Things began to change, however, when my mom found a passion and my dad became a hero.

After much thought, my mom decided to go to college and pursue a degree in education. Though it was often stressful, the work gave my mom purpose and, for one of the fist times in my life, I knew that she was truly happy. Around the same time, my paramedic father received word that a police officer was down in the midst of a hostage situation. Arriving at the house embroiled in gunfire and violence, my dad and his partner, Joe, realized that the fallen police officer, who had been shot multiple times, was going to die if they did not act quickly. Under heavy and continuous gunfire, with the help of his partner, my father crawled to the officer and began administering aid. Stuffing the officers' ripped open guts and intestines with towels, they were able to slow the bleeding enough to pull him out of harm's way. As they did, my father felt a sharp pain in his back and thought it was a bee. They rushed the officer to the hospital and, after a few hours, it became apparent they had saved his life. My father asked a physician about his wounds and realized that he had taken several pieces of shrapnel to his back. After his treatment, newsmen swarmed my father and begged for his account of the events. Through such exposure, dad became a hero. Later, he was awarded numerous honors for his role in the events, including Georgia Paramedic of the Year and one of the National Firefighters of the Year. After my mom found purpose and my dad became a hero, I think my parents fell back in love and, though my dad still struggled with alcohol and my mom with anger, the talk of divorce stopped. The nightmares also stopped. God spoke to me in these trying times and I realized that the dark experiences of evil, hardship and struggle often lead us to our most joyous mornings. Sometimes in life, we like Jesus, must go through the desert.

In the spring of third grade, I met one of the best friends I could have ever asked for, Newton Jackson. Everyday at recess, we led our team (or the group of kids we ran around with). Perhaps it was a friendship of convenience at first, he being black and I being white, we could unite a bunch of people in our class through joint leadership, but it grew into something much more beautiful. Our first joint operation was to plan for the battle of all battles against the other team (pretty much the rest of the class) on the playground in late March. We drew maps and formulated plans of attack.

I spent the night at Newton's house and he at mine numerous times to plan further. These dreaming and planning sessions led to many long talks about life and our families late at night. One night, I asked Newton, "Do you like girls?" "No, I like the feeling of being close to and up against boys better," he responded. Throughout our friendship, which lasted for about two more years, Newton made comments like these consistently. I often didn't really know what to make of them. Ultimately, when the day came to engage the other team, we were all in our respective positions, Newton and I gave the command, "Charge!" We met the other team on the field of battle or the kickball field, whichever you prefer. Our plan was masterful and, immediately as we overcame the other team, we both knew it. Just when I thought the battle was over, Samantha came up and kissed me. I sat there stunned. Then, I felt a sharp strike across my face that sent me to the ground. As I laid there dazed and confused, I knew I was in love.

Like any good evangelical, I learned early that defending myself and fighting was divine. This lesson did not come natural for a scrawny kid like me. In second and third grade, a huge older kid that rode my bus named Tom bullied me. Everyday at the bus stop, he would push me on the ground, kick me, punch me, call me a pussy, and say that my dad was a faggot. When we got on the bus, he would hit me in the back of the head, give me wet willies, steal my lunch money and call me fish breath. When I saw him at school, he would tell everyone I smelled like poop, his dad would kill my dad and other niceties. I absolutely hated Tom and every night I prayed that God would deliver me from his clutches. By the end of third grade, God did.

One day, as we were riding the bus, I got called to the front. Mrs. Tankersly, our bus driver, told me that Tom had told her what I said. I didn't have any clue what she was talking about. "Tell the truth," she demanded, "Did you say that you wanted to stick your billy into Ansley's tutu?" Although I knew Ansley, I didn't know what these concoctions of words meant. I was 8! I told her that I didn't know what she was talking about. Nevertheless, she told my mom I was talking about sex on the bus. Thankfully, my mom knew that I didn't know anything about the subject and she defended me. Mrs. Tankersly lived across the street from us and, seeing her in her driveway, my mom decided to confront her about the situation. I listened from the upstairs window and could hear her well. "Jeffrey will not be riding the bus anymore…that's for damn sure…and don't you ever say such nasty things about my son anymore. You are the only nasty bitch in this situation! Get it?" It was the first time I had heard my mom use this word bitch, but it would not be the last. After these events, I told my parents about Tom having picked on me for the last two years. My dad told me that God always wanted me to defend myself and taught me the art of punching a bigger kid as hard as I could between the legs. He told me that he would be proud of me when I defended myself and would take me to Dairy Queen as a reward. I was a sugar fiend and so I loved the ending of this exhortation.

  It wasn't a few days later that friends of our family came by the house. I was playing with their youngest son, Charlie, who was my age and about five inches taller than me, in our basement. As we were playing war with G.I. Joes, he playfully hit me with a toy. For some reason, this set me off and all of my previous experiences with Tom came rushing back. I punched Charlie as hard as I could right between the legs. Then once he was down, I got on top of him and slugged him uncontrollably in the face. Then I bit him on his stomach and drew blood there too. As he was struggling to get up, I kicked him twice. Hysterically, he ran out of the room, blood running down his face, screaming for help from both his parents and mine. I took my time leaving the room. I was quite proud of myself, knew my dad would be proud too, and joyfully thanked God for giving me the strength to whip him. With my chest held out and knowing that I was going to get to go to Dairy Queen, I walked into the room were everyone else was. Much to my surprise, everyone looked at me with horror and my dad snatched me up to discipline me. As I was screaming, what about Dairy Queen, my dad gave me the worst spanking of my life. By the time I walked back out, the other family had left. For the next few days, I worked on a letter of apology to Charlie and his family. I knew the only way out of the doghouse was to talk about how the devil had taken over my body, how I was begging them and God for forgiveness and to tell them how much I truly loved them. It worked. By the next time I saw Charlie, he still had a patch on his forehead from the beating, but he was really nice to me. Through all of these experiences, I began to wonder if violence was worth the cost.

I had some weird interactions with church leaders growing up. I remember this one guy named Joey, who was known for dressing up at every event for kids as "Bubbles the Clown." Us kids loved him. We would cheer and jump around when he arrived at birthday parties, pool parties, holiday parties and other events. Bubbles made balloons, sang songs, danced around and led us in all types of mischief. One day, after a particularly fun church pool and water fight party, us boys went to the bathroom to change. Bubbles, I guess, was the self-appointed watchmen to make sure that we didn't drown each other in the toilets or get in too big of fights. As we were changing in the bathroom, I remember looking up and seeing Bubbles licking his lips with an incredibly strange look on his face. Although I thought it very odd, I just put my clothes on a little quicker and got out of the room. I forgot about the situation. A few weeks later, the Sheriff's Department came to my school to do a presentation on predators and child molestation. The deputies were very careful with their wording, as most of us didn't know anything about sex, much less sex or sexuality with children. They talked about needing to run away and report it when adults offered us candy for favors, asked us to sleep with them or had odd interactions with us when we were naked. The deputies told us, if we had any concerns, we should inform our teachers.

Later that day, one of the boys in my class asked me at lunch if I knew any predators, I replied that I thought I might and his name is Bubbles. The following year, I thought about what the deputies said at school when we were at the local church camp and the director, Todd, showered with us and watched all of us intently. I thought it odd when he commented to one of the boys, "You really look like a big boy naked." During the school year, this man was the children's director for our local church association. Though weird and out of the norm, I never thought that these events rose to the level of what the deputies were talking about, at least until I got older.

Death was always talked about at our church. The phrase "dying and going to hell" was used about as much as the name "Jesus" was. I knew both older and younger people who were dying. I always wondered where they went. I also wondered where I was going too. I had always loved Jesus, but thought that God would inevitably make him send me to hell, because I was often a bad kid. For me, throughout my earliest years, death was synonymous with hell. I always thought Jesus was the good cop, God was the bad cop and the Holy Ghost was like Casper the Friendly Ghost. I didn't really get the whole trinity thing. These consistent discussions and my belief that I was inevitably going to hell caused thoughts of death and dying to terrify me. One night, after having dinner with family friends at Longhorn's Steakhouse, our family drove back through town and arrived at an intersection filled with devastation. I knew it wasn't a random car accident. The cars were on top of each other and the red light was smashed on the ground. My dad asked a police officer he knew at the scene what was going on. "Jeff a damned tornado just came through and killed three people." I was stunned and began to softly cry. This is the moment that the mania surrounding tornadoes entered my life. Later that night, I couldn't sleep for fear that destined for hell, I too was going to be taken up and killed in a tornado. I was scared, would start shaking, feel pains in my chest and I simply couldn't make it stop. This was the first of about five months of such nights. During the day at school, I had trouble doing my schoolwork, even when it was sunny outside, because I thought a tornado was going to hit. Throughout the spring and summer, I refused to go outside to play at recess or at home. I would become physically ill if I was forced to. I just knew that death by a tornado was always imminent. The preacher's consistent exhortations about hell always made me think that there was no way Jesus could ever save me…God's desire to damn me was just too strong. I knew the tornado was going to be the vessel that took me there.

    Late one night, our dog Magic had puppies in our backyard. We didn't even know she was pregnant and only realized she was in labor when we heard her moaning. Looking back, I guess she was just cruising around the neighborhood. After practicing some amateur veterinary medicine, dad took us out into our backyard to see the new arrivals. There were eight of them and one was particularly smaller than the others. Dad said that this was the runt and probably wouldn't make it through the night. This sent me into a crisis. I didn't want anything to die. The only thought that consoled me was to think about the words of our preacher, "Animals don't go to heaven." These words made me think that at least I would have a dog to offer me companionship as I suffered in hell after dying in the tornado.

    I remained afraid of being alone. When I went to bed at night, I would quietly listen for everyone who was still awake. Their noises were my salvation. I somehow figured that if I could hear them then my family was still alive and I was not dead. Most nights, after I could tell that my mom and dad had gone to bed, I slipped into my parent's room to make sure multiple times a night that they were still alive. On more than one occasion, I got the shock of my life when I saw my parents engaged in what seemed to be naked wrestling. I had no idea that they practiced the moves of the World Wrestling Federation at night. The next morning they would always act awkward. I guess they knew that I knew their wrestling secret.

Regardless, after slipping by their room to see if they were asleep or wrestling, I would go to my brother's room and wake him up. While there, I would beg my brother to sleep in the same bed with me. Sometimes I bribed him with my week's allowance. The going rate was about two dollars per night. That was a lot considering our allowance was often our age. Nevertheless, I was incredibly grateful that my brother would come sleep with me. When he got in the bed, I scooted my foot over to touch him. I figured that if he died or I died I would be able to feel it. I was able to go to sleep with this arrangement. It made me feel safe. Then came what we called the night terrors. My brother, for some unbeknownst reason, started occasionally and lucidly arising in the middle of the night thrashing with tears and blood curtailing screams. In the morning, he would not remember having the fits and the pediatrician said that kids often have them as a sort of growing pain. The night terrors really scared me, because my brother was acting like the demons that the preacher at church had spoke of and described. In fact, the first time it happened, I got in trouble for punching my brother in the face in the middle of the night. I figured I was getting a visit from the demons and had to fight them off for now. Needless to say, it was fairly intense to wake up to this type of activity in your bed. The night terrors only happened about three times a month and I was so scared of death, God, and hell that I took my chances for a good night's rest on the other twenty seven other days. The fears pushed me to say the sinner's prayer over and over again when I would go to sleep. There were nights were I prayed the prayer hundreds of times in a row.

The Great Awakening

Are our seeing eyes blind?

I grew up in the midst of a great awakening. Evangelicals were exploding in growth. Our church was at the center of the storm. Our pastor, Brother Todd, was perhaps the best mix of kindness and harshness that I had ever seen. Humorously, he went to the same seminary that I later did. On a personal level, Todd was always friendly and present in times of tragedy or struggle. On a pastoral level, he was a culture warrior and spoke of our church being in a tremendous battle for the heart of our nation. I often found this strange, as I saw no mention of our nation in the Bible. Nevertheless, one of Brother Todd's favorite things to preach about was our eternal destiny. He would go into the sermon and have you imagining fire coming down from heaven to destroy you, God sitting on his throne of judgment and turning you away, tragic accidents in which you never have the chance to accept Jesus, the possibility of your death before you even left the service, the eternal judgment that awaited every false step here on earth and many of other less than pleasant thoughts. When I later heard about and learned of the sermons of Jonathon Edwards, making people stand on the backs of their pews for fear of hell, I thought that cat couldn't hold a candle to our Brother Todd. He would pack them into our sanctuary and sermonicly make them feel the fires of hell tickling their toes. By the end of his sermon, everyone was always on edge. The service always ended with the same exhortation. "Will this be the last time that you get the chance to accept Jesus? Please friend, don't let Jesus let go of you. He is calling... Will you answer?" As *Just As I Am* played softly on the organ and piano, Brother Todd asked for every head bowed and every eye to be closed. He then began to lead us in his version of the Sinner's Prayer..."Lord, I am the most wretched vile disgusting filthy sinner the world has ever known. I know that I am lost and going to hell without you. Please, please, please Lord in your infinite mercy save me from this most wretched and frightening of destinies. I accept you and hope that you will accept me and allow me into your kingdom." By no means the most affirming of prayers. Then the middle part, as the music began to play louder, "Now, it is time to complete the process of salvation...Jesus says that if you do not acknowledge me before men, I will not acknowledge you in heaven...We invite those who have accepted Christ today to complete the process." I said the prayer every week and was often too distracted by looking to see who else would walk down the aisle to go myself. Honestly, I was always too scared. I remember being baffled that the same people would come down the aisle every time and I just assumed it must not have taken the first time. No matter who walked down, Brother Todd would say the same thing, "Now only they know their own hearts...whether they are truly repentant or not...only they know...but upon their profession of faith we offer them membership into our church." Again, by no means the most affirming of statements. No matter how many there were or how many times they came down before, the church always stood to clap.

    My family would leave church and marvel about how many persons got saved on the walk to the car in the parking lot. From these conversations, I realized that church was often a numbers game. Then we would pull out and every Sunday as we passed the workers at the plant nursery, owned by a Jewish family, across the street, my dad would yell the same thing, "Get to church!" I always thought that such antics were weird when we were supposed to be witnessing to them. Sunday dinners were filled with fried chicken, black-eyed peas, candied yams and discussion of who walked down the aisle again and how they must be having an affair to feel that much guilt. The gossip was endless, salacious, and entertaining...my brother and I loved it. The more dramatic it got...the more excited we got. I always loved the criticisms of my grandfather who never went to church with us. Sometimes, I thought for sure he was going to hell. I told him so too. During the summer, my other grandmother asked me if I had ever truly gotten saved and I replied, "Yes, about 15 times." She then said, "Well then you never truly meant it." As the crowds got larger and the church filled to capacity, Brother Todd's exhortations got more intense. Now, I was not as sure as I once was and really began to worry.

Doubts

Life is a series of uncertainties.

By the spring of 1992, I was really struggling. As every small gust of wind beckoned the next tornado and every sermon brought the fires of hell closer, I was finishing up the third grade and quickly losing my mind, soul and spirit. I spent many afternoons looking at the other kids playing on the playground and wondered about my eternal destiny. As I thought about dinosaurs and the origins of evil, I realized for the first time in my life that I was more of a doubter than a believer. Since everyone else, including my parents and my teachers at the church, seemed so certain about God, Jesus and the Bible, I figured I would bring my questions to them.

One day sitting in class at church, my teacher, Mrs. Cynthia, was describing all the beautiful animals that were quietly and loving getting-along with Adam and Eve in the Garden of Eden. As everyone else cooed, my mind began to race. Then Mrs. Cynthia exhibited the beautiful illustrations of fierce lions, soft lambs, beautiful birds, gigantic whales, nice snakes and every other creature you could imagine all gently and peacefully walking, slithering, swimming and flying around as if in some type of parade. I got the courage to speak, "Oh yeah, well what about the dinosaurs?" When all of the teachers in the class suddenly frighteningly and menacingly looked my way, I knew I had said something disruptive and disturbing. Mrs. Cynthia replied, "Well of course we know that there were no dinosaurs in the Garden of Eden." I quickly and rebelliously replied back, "Well you said that all the animals of the earth were there. We learned at school that there are all types of dinosaurs. What about the T-Rex? How in the world could all of those animals get along when some were carnivores and needed meat to survive?" Mrs. Cynthia was befuddled and finally answered, "Dinosaurs have never existed!" I knew this was false. As my heart began to race, I pushed further, "What about the fossils we have seen pictures of at school?" It seemed crazy to me to think that everything I was being told at school was a lie. Mrs. Cynthia got more desperate and blurted out, "God put the bones and fossils in place to test our faith." All of the other kids were mystified by this brazen display of courage and rebellion. I continued questioning, "Does the Bible ever speak of dinosaurs? If not, then how can we know that it is telling us anything about our history?" Eventually, one of the other teachers, Mr. Frank, who also happened to be a good friend of our family, silenced me by grabbing me and taking me out of the room. When we got outside, he demandingly asked of me, "What was all of that in there? You are damaging the faith of the other kids. Do you believe in Jesus son? Are you saved?" Like most kids, my response to such harshness was to hang my head low, shut up and begin to cry. I felt a fiery hotness come to my face and my heart began to race. I went to the bathroom and felt like I was going to die. It had happened before. Now, I realize that I was having a panic attack. When I got home, I got in big trouble for disrupting my class and being disrespectful to my teachers. As my father spanked me, he said, "This is because I love you and God loves you." As was often the pattern in our family, questions of doubt were met with a swift rebuke. In this and other moments, I was taught that my doubts were damaging to others.

    A few weeks later, I began to timidly ask my parents further questions that I had. I softened my approach. I started to ask about evil and God. I saw on television all the wars, famines, deaths, robberies and bad things going on and wanted to know why. My parents, who seemed quite sure of God, goodness and life, seemed like they, as the authority figures in my life, might have some answers. I asked my dad first, "Where does evil come from?" He responded with an exhortation to go and ask your mother. I sheepishly asked my mom, as she had been known to fly off into a rage over perceived disrespect, the same question, "Where does evil come from?" "Satan of course!" she knowingly replied. I kept going. "Well who created Satan?" She had a comeback for this too, "God created him as an angel and he rebelled...that's what the Bible says." "If God knows everything, then why did God create him in the first place?" "Go to your room!" came her final reply. As I walked to my room, I realized that she didn't know and, furthermore, didn't want to entertain the questions or conversation. As I laid down in my bed, I began to earnestly pray, "Lord, I don't know what the answers are, but I want you to be the answer...Please, Lord, reveal yourself and help me with my questions." The revelation and answers I desperately sought didn't seem to come.

After this incident, I began to ask people that I thought might be sympathetic about my conundrum. Most were not. The kids at church taunted me. Stephanie demanded, "Do you know that you are going to hell without Jesus?" The kids were getting their first crack at witnessing and often mimicked the pastor. Paul inquired, "If you were to die tonight, do you know what would happen to you?" Others took the concerned approach, "I am worried about you...as I don't think you have asked Jesus into your heart?" Some were often more brash and mean. Jessica spoke down to me, "You are an idiot for not having accepted Jesus yet." My church was very good at educating the youngest amongst us to follow the teachings of salvation, witnessing, hell and damnation. One day though, things changed when I asked one of the kinder ladies in the church, Mrs. Janice, about God. She told me, "Jesus is love and love is Jesus. God is love and love is God." I was amazed. I thought back to the picture of my youth, with all of the children sitting around Jesus, and knew that this was the Jesus that I wanted to know...the one of love. I began to ask more questions.

    One day, riding in the car with my mom, next to the small ponds close to my grandparents house, I made a bold declaration, which I thought would be welcomed with open arms, "Mom I am ready to get saved and baptized...just like the preacher asks us to." Using a tactic that many parenting experts in the evangelical community thought would be helpful in increasing certainty, making kids work for their parents permission to be saved, my mom demurred, "You're not old enough." I was devastated and kept demanding, "I am ready to get saved!" After a few months of going back and forth, I attended Vacation Bible School (for Southern Baptists...VBS). I was so happy that my teacher was Mrs. Janice, as she loved the God of love. The week was beautiful and filled with stories of Jesus' healing, helping, loving and sacrificing for all people. On the final day of class, she told us of Jesus conquering death, coming back from the grave, and loving us so much that he would never leave us. I knew I wanted whatever she was selling. Mrs. Janice prayed with me and told my mom that I was ready to get saved.

Throughout the week, I went to Vacation Bible School in the mornings and the basketball camp in the afternoons. There was only a thirty-minute gap between the two for lunch. Having only thirty minutes, my mom acted quickly. I guess she felt that my eternal destiny hung in the balance. Sitting on the steps in our split-level house, she asked me to follow her lead. Though I had heard it many times before, I followed her every word. "Lord Jesus I know that I am a sinner and in need of you…" "Lord Jesus I know that I am a sinner and in need of you…" "I want you to come into my heart…" "I want you to come into my heart…" "Grant me assurance of my salvation that I might will live forever with you." "Grant me assurance of my salvation that I might live forever with you." When we finished, I was overwhelmed with joy. My mom congratulated me and told me that I was now her brother in Christ. I wondered if this would stop some of the chores, hurtful statements and oppressive behaviors I had consistently been subjected to. Nevertheless, I was so happy that I had finally met this God of love. On the way to basketball camp, my mom called one of her friends, "I got him to VBS, saved and now to basketball camp...we are rolling over here at our house." For some reason, the nonchalant nature of my mother's remarks made the whole experience feel cheapened.

When I got to basketball camp, I excitedly told one of my friends, Trey, from church that I had met Jesus today and got saved. His remark came swift and like a knife plunging into my chest, "So what...I got saved three years ago when I was in first grade. You are so stupid, what took you so long?" The next week, I finally walked down the aisle and proclaimed that I knew Christ to the church. At the very least, if Brother Todd was right, I felt that Jesus would see my confession before men and confess me before his father in heaven. A few months later, when Brother Todd came by the house, he kept asking me the same question over and over again, "Do you know that you know that you know Jesus son?" After a few wrong answers, exasperated, I finally and firmly replied, "I met Jesus in June and am ready to be baptized."

Our new Sunday school classes always began in August and my main teacher for the year was Mrs. Lefa. She was a kind, generous and gentle woman who taught me consistently of the love of God. The date of my baptism was set for August 30, as my church, unlike the Church of Christ, didn't feel the need to rush things, due to the fact that fear and uncertainty kept the coffers full. In late August, I brought my swimsuit, towel, and change of clothes to Sunday school class with me. Mrs. Lefa encouraged me in the big step that I was taking and I walked downstairs to the sanctuary with my dad. When the time came, I lowered myself into the water to meet Brother Todd. As hundreds watched the ceremony, I confessed my faith in Jesus and was baptized in the waters. I was really scrawny and squirmy little kid and I guess Brother Todd wasn't used to baptizing salamanders. As he put me under, I slipped out of his hands and my feet went in the air. Everyone in the audience laughed and, when I came up, I swam to the other side to meet my dad. I guess mom's early swimming lessons had come in handy. When I returned to church, my mom slipped me a present, my first devotional book, which had been inscribed with love from my parents. I was now a real Christian! Maybe?

Lessons

Learning is scary.

It wasn't a few months after the summer's salvific events that the nightmares crept back in. By now, I was speeding through the later years of elementary school. My teacher, Mrs. Charles, had the strangest demeanor I had ever known. I got in trouble a lot at school that year due to the fact that I couldn't sleep at night for fear that I was going to hell. God and hell were always on my mind. For some reason, I thought that taking my grandfather's advice and beginning to act like a respectable Christian businessman would alleviate my fears and struggles. Still interested in politics, I championed the Republican Party to all who would listen. "Just wait until the midterm elections…Newt is going to win back the house." I told a bunch of clueless kids at school. I also became very concerned with the clothes that I wore to school. I wanted to look respectable and started wearing dress shirts to school everyday. On big days, I would bust out the tie. During this time, I purchased my first bottle of hair gel and started slicking back my hair. At lunch, everyone loved the mashed potatoes and I would sell mine for a dollar per portion. I also sold pencils and notebooks whenever I found a buyer. For a time, I was the don of the school. I was glad nobody knew that I was always scared to death at night and made my brother sleep with me for fear of God and hell.

    I played basketball and baseball. My dad always coached our teams and sometimes we were good. I learned many lessons in my interactions with the recreational leagues and rarely were they ever about sports. I was never all that good at basketball. I began playing in first grade and didn't score my first points until fourth grade. My dad always encouraged me. I knew that he was a big athlete in high school and I always wanted to be like him. One day on the way to a Saturday morning game, I heard on the radio that there was a big struggle in our home state of Georgia over the state flag. There was a Confederate Battle Flag on the flag and there was growing momentum to remove it. I knew that we were supposed to be on the side of the Confederates, because that was the side we always cheered for in the reenactment of the Battle of Jonesboro. I asked my dad what the fuss was all about, he remarked, "The blacks are just getting excited about something that doesn't matter…the Confederate Battle Flag is about our heritage not hate son." After we played the game, I was outside playing with a black friend and he asked me when

I thought that white people would stop flying the Confederate flag. Partial mimicking my dad, I replied, "I think that the blacks need to quite getting excited about it. It is about our heritage." After he went home, we never played together again. I thought about these events for a long time.

Later in the spring, I started playing baseball with the Cardinals. This was the first time that the pitcher was another kid and we were taking live swings from them. I was always scared of the ball and batted last. To say that I stunk would be an understatement. Before one game, a guy on my team saw a bright red cardinal fly on to the field and started getting really excited. He said that it was a sign of tremendous favor on our team. We ended up beating the Dodgers by eleven runs and, like the kid on my team, I began to believe in signs. As I struggled to believe, I prayed that God would show me the sign of the cross to let me know that God was there. I began to see crosses everywhere. These two lessons proved both impactful and difficult.

I experienced my first bout of heartbreak. My first love Jesse dumped me for a guy named Tim. I didn't feel like much of a don anymore and the whole situation made very angry. I told her I was mad. "You are the ugliest boy I have ever known," she graciously replied. As I daily watched Jesse and Tim hold hands on the playground, my heart broke over and over again. I felt like I was emulating one of my grandfather's soap operas. I pushed deeper into the questions of God.

I became very depressed once more and couldn't shack the feeling that Jesus hated me. When I saw a friend wearing a "Jesus Loves Me!" t-shirt, I thought well he doesn't love me or I wouldn't be dealing with all of this pain. Brother Todd's exhortations that we experience heartache when we haven't been faithful to God only made matters worse. One day I went to one of my church teachers to talk about my problems. She told me that she was getting divorced and that I didn't yet know real live pain and worry. There was constantly so much pain and fear at our church that people had a difficult time being empathetic or generous, even with little kids. I didn't have anybody to go too with all of these issues. Then it happened.

One day I stood up in the middle of class and declared, "I am an existentialist. I believe in existence and that is all." To be perfectly honest, I didn't know totally what that word meant. A few weeks prior, I heard it and looked it up in the dictionary. But growing tired of Jesus and hell, I declared that I believed in nothing more than existence. I knew I was lying. I prayed all the time, feared I wasn't truly saved and constantly saw the crosses. I wanted to believe in Jesus, but found myself in consistent dark fits of struggle with faith and reality. Back in the classroom, as I sat down, the teacher and entire class looked at me as if I had ripped off all my clothes and ran around the room. No one knew what to say. I felt strangely warm. Then, Mrs. Charles got up, said thank you, and continued on with class as if nothing ever happened. Later that night, my mom said that Mrs. Charles called and wanted to know if everything was ok at home. Mom exploded, "Why do you consistently embarrass us with these antics? Can you not just be a kid and stop trying to figure everything out?" I didn't know what to say. I knew she was stressed. I apologized.

During this time, my parents were busy. Mom was still going to school and working hard as ever to perfect the make-up of the latest project. I can remember many late nights with her grinding out the latest assignment by computer light. She stayed up late and worked incredibly hard. Fireman and paramedics often work twenty-four hours on and forty-eight hours off schedules. This gave my dad up to four extra days a week to pursue a second job. After getting tired of working for my overbearing grandfather, dad decided to start his own landscaping business. When summertime came and school got out, we would ride along and work extra hard picking weeds and cutting grass. Probably our biggest talent, though, was being able to find the largest patch of shade in the yard we were cutting and resting underneath. During all of this time, both of my parents were really stressed out. They oscillated between working too much and working on their marriage. I believe they were constantly victims of Brother Todd's exhortations to become Biblical scholars and expert Christians while working their tales off to give more money to the church and develop the perfect marriage that the church demanded. Us kids were not the most cooperative of partners in all of these endeavors.

My brother and I fought constantly. When I heard that Jesus came to bring a sword used as a metaphor for defending one's self and violence, I felt comfortable whipping my brother whenever he crossed me. I can remember two times that caused a tremendous stir. Once, my brother and I were at Wal-Mart shopping with my mom. We went straight to the magazines and began looking at the latest Sports Illustrated. There being one copy, we naturally got in a fight over who was going to read it. I speared my brother into a shelf and, before we knew it, it was an all out brawl. We went back and forth slamming each other into shelving. A woman in the aisle screamed, "Oh my God...Stop it! Please stop it!" We kept going and, as she tried to pull us off of each other, the top-shelve collapsed. As cans and boxes rained down on the woman and us, my mom came around the corner and screamed. She snatched us up and ran us to the car. I have always wondered what happened to that woman. On another occasion, we were out at the church playing basketball with my dad. While he played with the men, my brother and I got in a fight on the bleachers. It got nasty quickly. Finally, I had had enough and I picked up my brother over my head and threw him from the top bleacher. He landed on and deadened his two front baby teeth. For the next two years in our family pictures, my brother had two blackened front teeth. I know these were times of tremendous struggle for my parents. Divorce probably seemed like a reasonable option.

Though I was quite serious much of the time, I still did some normal kid things. During fourth grade, I really got into two things, video games and sewers. I had a Nintendo 64. I can remember opening the paper on Christmas morning and falling in love. Here was the machine that would make all of my dreams come true. I, strangely, thought that somehow the machine would be enough to take away all of my doubts and struggles. For awhile, it seemed to do the trick. My favorites were *Starfox*, World Wrestling Federation's *Wrestlemania* and Ken Griffey, Jr.'s *Homerun Baseball*. These games offered me an escape for one of the first times in my life. I was able to step into a virtual world and be somebody else. I flew through strange lands killing the bad guys, fought as Hulk Hogan and knocked homeruns as Ken Griffey, Jr. My dad played the baseball game with me and thinking about those days brings a smile to my face. Ultimately, I got good enough to beat him and after that he didn't want to play anymore. I am thankful everyday when I think about those games. Some days, I think they might have saved my life. When the visions of hell and terror woke me up in the middle of the night, I went to the games and somehow found solace in them. In the afternoons, there was a huge open storm drain right next to our house and my brother and I loved playing in it. We would go in and crawl until we got to the smaller street drains. Our next-door neighbor George would hide across the street and whistle when people were about to walk by. We terrified people daily with our antics and loved every minute of it. For some reason, we never worried about snakes or anything else that could be living in there. Video games and sewers offered me brief joy in the midst of the hellish thoughts that flooded my brain.

Although I had learned much, the real education didn't begin until the summer. We had a crab-apple tree. Little green apples fell from it and practically flooded our backyard. My brother and I loved throwing the rotten ones at each other, as they often exploded on contact. One day, my best friend Trey, who was about two years older, came over. We climbed the tree as high as we could go. There, perched up in the sky, Trey asked me one of the most enlightening questions I have ever known, "Do you want to know about sex?" I paused. I didn't know what to do. I knew that sex was a bad word and it was as if Trey had offered me a piece of forbidden fruit. My mind wondered back to the Garden of Eden and I thought, "Maybe this is exactly what Satan offered Eve?" Timidly, I said yes, knowing that there would be no turning back. I wondered if I too would be banished from God for learning about this phenomenon that Brother Todd consistently railed against. Trey told me of insertions and vaginas, explaining using stark imagery. I was floored. Never before had I heard of such things and I am surprised that I didn't fall flat out of the tree.

When the summer came, my parents decided that we needed a membership at a pool. For many years, we swam every summer at a family friend's house. Then, something happened to stop the swimming, which I think had to do with my mother throwing the family's decked out oldest daughter in the pool before a big date. Regardless, I was really excited about the pool. It offered fun in the sun, a clubhouse, tennis courts and an awesome picnic area. One day, when we were swimming, a family we were close to brought a black friend from school to the pool. We had been playing together for a long time, when the owner of the pool's red truck came zooming up. He opened the door of his truck and ran up screaming, "Get out! Get out! There are no niggers allowed in this pool!" The little girl began to cry. We couldn't believe it. Packing up all of our things, we left the pool with the little girl and vowed to never come back. I felt sick and cried. Later that night, dad led us in a prayer for the little girl and the old racist. I began to realize what loving my enemies looked like. In my dreams that night, I dreamed that God was a black female who was holding the black girl and I close to keep us safe. I still love that dream.

On July the Fourth, we went to a party at my aunt's house. I loved riding down to the country and playing in the cornfields and pastures with my cousins. My parents always adorned us in our finest clothes and gold chains to illustrate how well we were doing financially. I knew better. I had heard the arguments over maxed out credit cards and the need to stop spending. In the country, things seemed simpler. We played all day. Then, as evening fell, things began to get complicated. My brother pulled down his pants to his ankles and began peeing on a decorative felted cross on the back porch. I guess he thought he was outside and wasn't paying attention to where he was aiming. Nevertheless, my grandmother screamed, "He's peeing on Jesus! He's peeing on Jesus! Stop him! Stop him!" She ran to grab my brother and, turning him around, he started peeing on her feet. Chaos ensued and, before I knew it, we had both gotten spankings for the incident, Justin for peeing and me for laughing.

About an hour after the chaos, a kid who was just visiting with one of my cousins began to taunt my brother and pushed him down. I got pissed and then attacked the boy. Holding his head down, I punched and bit him. My chuch teacher said that Jesus always defended himself and, though at the time I questioned his assertion based on the cross, in this moment I found this to be my theology too. Blood squirted from the little boy's bite mark and, before I knew it, I was getting another spanking.

My grandmother remarked that my brother and I had not been raised right. My mom got pissed and, before I knew it once more, we were back in the car on the way home. The next day, we had baseball games. It was a tough day. Both my brother and my team lost. As we were getting in the car, my mom noticed a lady a few cars over slamming a child's head against the steering wheel. My mom jumped out of the car and demanded that the woman stop. When the lady came up, I recognized her. She was the mom of Jonny...a kid from my class the previous school year. My mother distracted her and this allowed the child enough time to get free. Running to the car, my mom barely made it in and locked the doors, before the woman tried to tackle her. The woman, laying on top of the hood of the car as my mom pulled out, was screaming, "Get out of the car and fight me like a real woman you bitch…I know you got my license plate." The woman then stood in front of all of the cars as people honked for her to move. As my mom revved her engine and threatened to kill her, my brother and I sat scared in the back seat in total shock. Eventually, the woman moved. Jonny wasn't in my school anymore the next year. I learned lessons about the world in those days.

Fifth grade began with a bang. The Sunday before school started, Brother Todd stood up in front of the congregation and announced his resignation. My heart grew strangely warm. I was tired of the fear and ready for something new. I still wanted to believe in Jesus, but the fear of him that I felt was incredibly powerful. Faith was and is a tough place for me. One of the older men in the church who had consistently spoken of his "hate for the niggers that were starting to come to the church" over the years had a tragic accident. Unable to hear, he drove his convertible onto the train tracks. The man was rendered incapacitated. I thought my racist grandfather was next. Since Brother Todd had always talked about reaping what we sow, I actually expected all of the racists to be incapacitated soon.

Between Brother Todd giving his one-month notice and leaving, the Royal Ambassadors of the church took all of us boys on a trip to Camp Deer Pass. We were there for two days. The first night we had a huge bonfire with thousands of other kids. It was amazing. The fire was the size of a small house. Then the evangelist came out to tell all of us kids about the lake of fire spoken of in Revelation. He said that if we didn't accept Jesus, that we would all burn in a fire like the one in front of us, for eternity. Something in the fire exploded as he uttered these words, undoubtedly put there on purpose. As the flames crashed, the minister begged us to accept Jesus and save ourselves from the fate of hell that awaits all who reject Him. For one of the first times in my life, though scared, I resisted. I felt like these tactics were not about God and I felt like the whole situation was a charade.

Later that night, we slept out in the woods. After the adults went to bed in their cars, we all began to creep at of our tents and run around wild in the woods. It was as if a pack of hyenas had been hibernating and were now unleashed. Eventually, the adults caught us and forced us to go to bed. I found it strange that the kid who was getting in trouble the most was the kid who had little money and ratty clothes visiting our church from another town. The next day we took a hike to the huge Indian mounds. While there, our head guide opened the floor for questions. I leadingly inquired, "What ever happened to the Indians who made this mound?" The guide quickly explained, "As they all got tired of being close to cities...they peacefully packed up and took trains to happily live on pieces of land given to them by the government." As he was trying to change the subject, I demanded, "You know we all go to school and have heard about the Trail of Tears...it seems to me that you are exploiting these people by charging us to take this tour." One of the men from our church snatched me up and took me to the side, "What are you doing??? There is nothing Christian about the way you are acting." Over the summer, my interest in Dr. Martin Luther King, Jr., Bobby Kennedy and the prophet Jeremiah peaked. I knew from reading their stories that Christians were supposed to speak out against injustice. I replied, "The Christian thing to do is to speak...the United States terrorized and killed the Indians. Why can't he just say that?" The leader grew increasingly agitated and red, "Boy, I served our nation in the Marine Corp and God will punish you for speaking out against his federal government. The United States is God's righteous and chosen nation. For right now, you just stop talking until we get home. I want you to think about your salvation." I obliged the man and rode the bus silently for the two-hour trip home. I was hurt. When we got home, as I waited for my mom, I thought about the fire, the Indians, the leader and grew worried.

My mom's maroon Honda Accord pulled up to the church and I got in the front seat. We pulled out and my mom asked, "How was the trip?" I didn't want to talk. "Fine," I demurred. "Are you sure you don't want..." My mom's voice trailed off as the glass crashed and the door was pushed in. I went unconscious for a few seconds and, when I awoke, I saw the mangled truck hood of the other car next to me and heard my mom screaming and yelling for me to be ok. Blood ran down my face and I assumed that I was dying. "Hurry! This is a direct relative of Jeff Hood," I kept hearing. In my mind, I knew why this was happening, because according to Brother Todd, God always punishes us for our sins. I knew, at Camp Deer Pass, I had rebelled against God and the teachings of the church. This was my punishment. At the hospital, the doctors said that I just had a bad gash on my forehead and I knew that God had spared me. Brother Todd cheerfully came to see me at the hospital and I didn't know whom I was more scared of, him or the doctors digging at my forehead. I went home, thanked God for forgiving my sins, and promised to never rebel against our church's teachings again. Brother Todd and his family tearfully completed their service to our church the next Sunday. As we traveled through the receiving line to thank them, Brother Todd cheerfully remarked to my mother, "You are the meanest woman I have ever known!" My mom really respected Brother Todd and, though he seemed to be kidding, I knew the remark really hurt her feelings. At home, she cried.

I knew that it was going to be a long year at school on the first day. When my mother found out that I was in Ms. Smith's fifth grade class, she was ticked and demanded, "How could you put my gifted son in the class of the ditto queen?" Dittos, for those who don't know, were the purple looking worksheets that teachers handed out to keep kids busy. I experienced a ton of pressure in those days to make good grades. From the beginning though, I knew I didn't like Ms. Smith. There was a space the teacher called Antarctica where the bad kids were forced to sit (alone in the corner of the room). I decided that was where I wanted to sit all the time.

As most of the kids made fun of me, I sat in the corner of the room and quietly did my work. Two kids were particularly brutal, Daniel and Dontell. Daniel took my ice cream money everyday and kicked my feet out from under me on the playground. Dontell always messed with me when I was in the bathroom. One of the few places of solace that I found was in quietly reading Goosebumps books by R.L. Stine. In these scary stories, I learned to respect and commune with the odd and paranormal. I became a strange kid quickly. Throughout the fall, I constructed a cemetery on the playground outside for dead pets. I told everyone in my class that I came in the night and buried pets. I instructed them not to mess with me or I would call forth the spirits of the pets to eat them. I swore that there was a pet tiger in there. This made Daniel and Dontell subside for a little while. Then things kicked back up. By early November, after the tortuous bullying, I broke. Ms. Smith refused to proactively stop the bullying and I got tired of it. To get her back, I decided that I would steal all of the candy that she gave out for prizes to the class for good behavior. I filled my book bag with as much as it could hold. When school got out, I went to the library. As I waited on my grandparents to pick me up, I knew that I had gotten away with it. Then, Ms. Smith came running into the room and demanded that I open my bag. I ran and eventually she caught me. Dramatically, she snatched my bag from me and candy fell all over the floor. I knew I was caught. When I got home, Ms. Smith had already called and my mom was devastated. She just knew that her oldest son had turned into a criminal. Due to these activities, I got the belt and was forced to go to counseling. While I talked to the counselor, she asked repeatedly, "Do you know Jesus son?"

    I began to have the poundings in my chest. I just knew that I was going to get left behind or banished to hell. I slept terrified that I was about to experience my palpitation here on earth. Throughout the misery, I tossed, turned and prayed for

God to make it stop. All I could hear was the sound of silence. The church's consistent exhortations of getting saved only made things worse. I accepted and believed over and over again...yet the paralyzing fear remained. One of the only bright spots came at church in late November. I was groggy when I arrived. I sat down at the table and waited on class to start. Some other kids started filling in the other chairs, until in walked a smiling Nelson Percy or more pejoratively Bible Man. Over the years, Nelson had always been the kid certain of his salvation, his knowledge of the Bible and his superior relationship to God. If there was ever a miniature or pint-sized Brother Todd, it was Nelson. On this day, Nelson looked like he was going to explode with either pure joy or oppressive Christian arrogance...I have always found it difficult to differentiate between the two. The class began and we talked about Jesus calling the disciples to be fishers of men. After a few minutes, Nelson couldn't hold it in any longer. He exploded, "I heard the voice of God last night!" The rest of us were just as curious as the teacher and longingly asked, "What did he say?" Nelson paused to allow the drama to build a bit, "Well guys...God told me that I needed to be a minister." The teacher then asked the wrong question, "Where were you?" He proudly replied with stiffness in his voice, "I can't believe it guys, but he spoke to me while I was laying in the bathtub."

The teacher smiled awkwardly. All of us boys had been holding it in, when my buddy asked, "Are you sure it wasn't your penis talking to you?" The teacher strongly rebuked us for laughing. We were quiet for a second and then she made a remark, "It is going to be very hard for Nelson to follow..." We lost it again. One girl asked Nelson, "How hard was it to hear those words?" By this point, the male helper in the class marched us all outside and angrily told us that the devil had a hold of our bodies. "Satan will you drag crude little boys to hell to suffer with him...ya'll minions are well on your way," he pushed further. We stood outside and expectantly waited on our parents to come get us. Most of us were too scared to move, yet one little boy got the courage to run away and meet his parents in another part of the church. When my dad picked me up and heard part of the story, I could tell by his slight smile while disciplining me that he thought it was funny too. Thankfully or unthankfully, depending on your perspective, Nelson is now a Southern Baptist pastor. Whatever spoke to him, I guess it was right.

    The Christmas season brought many new revelations. Right after Thanksgiving, we were told that Brother Todd's replacement had been found. I found myself terrified that something worse was coming. I just knew that this new pastor would make things worse. I kept asking for new video games in anticipation of needed relaxation. The weekend came. On Saturday, it was our responsibility as church members to go and meet the pastor. His name was Brother Donnie. I walked up to shake his hand in our church's meticulously adorned gathering room and asked, "How often do you talk about hell?" He laughed and responded, "Son, you can't talk about heaven without talking about hell." I knew we were in for more of the same. That night I struggled with his statement and wondered, "Is heaven that bound to the existence of hell?" The answer for most people I knew and my parents was…yes. It was devastating to think that a God of love and grace in heaven couldn't exist apart from a fallen angel of death and destruction in hell. The thought still plagues me.

    The next morning, we excitedly went to church to hear Brother Donnie's first sermon. It was the middle of the Christmas season. I expected a rousing sermon about the coming birth of Christ. Instead, Brother Donnie talked about the dangers of rejecting the newborn Christ like King Herod did. I moved to the end of my seat. I knew Brother Donnie was speaking directly to my salvation. I had rejected Christ so many times and sinned. Would I do it again? As Brother Donnie talked about parents not being able to take there kids to heaven, he asked for us to make a move of faith. "Will you pray with me? God I know that I am a wretched and vile sinner like Herod. Forgive me of my sins and bring me into a relationship with you." I prayed the prayer once again. I knew what was next. "Jesus says that those who deny me before men I will deny before my father in heaven..." As we sang *Come Just As You Are*, the invitation opened. "Come just as you are...feel the spirit call...don't wait until it's too late!" Brother Donnie demanded. I decided to go to the altar and pray. I felt this was a worthy compromise. I prayed the prayer of sinners two times before I sat back down. Surely, I thought I now know that I know Jesus and will get some relief. I sat back down and, before I could even take my seat, I felt the doubts and pain creep back in.

Though I prayed, I knew that not much had been accomplished. I missed the God of love, but she just seemed so distant now. Brother Donnie got a big surprise in his first week of ministry at our church. One of the church's big movers and shakers named Randolph Johnson up and left his wife. This would have been big enough news, but shortly after, he left his wife a note stating the real reason, "I have been a practicing gay man for most of my life and I can't hide it anymore." I knew Randolph to be one of the nicest guys at our church and a very godly man. My dad had always said similar things. When the decision and revelation went down though, everybody's attitudes dramatically changed. Now, he was vile and wretched. Everyone said they knew all along that he was sweet. At church, we weren't even allowed to speak his name. I didn't get the hypocrisy of it all and even the initial reason. The truth was that I didn't know what it meant to be gay or a homosexual. A few days later, in the midst of the Christmas shopping rush, I asked my mom. She said it was when two guys or two girls got together and urged, "It is unnatural, immoral, sinful, wrong and gross...don't you be getting any ideas." I was astonished. I began to think that this was what was going on with my best friend Newton Jackson, before he moved away. Ultimately, it was as if Randolph ceased to exist. We ran into him at the mall a few years later, as my mom tried to avoid him, he ran up and hugged us, he was the same old Randolph, just as nice, kind and generous as ever had been. He was much more like Jesus than most of the other folks at church I knew.

As the Christmas season continued, I began to wonder about toys and the coming of Santa. My mom always said that if we didn't believe then we wouldn't get any gifts. So, even in fifth grade, I professed belief. Unfortunately, over the years, the influx of gifts and the competition between my parents and grandparents for Christmas supremacy had often overshadowed the birth of Jesus. When Christmas Eve came, we went to church as we always had, it was a beautiful service and I found myself sublime looking at the porcelain baby in the manger who represented hope for the world. After church, we went over to my grandparents house. After a big feast, we began to open up all of the gifts. New shoes, video games, clothes and everything else were hidden underneath red wrapping paper. The next morning, we woke up to other mounds of gifts that had been placed in our living room. As was custom, my mom left a half-eaten banana and cookie to signify Santa's arrival and departure. She truly did always try to make Christmas as special as possible. When we got to my grandparents house for lunch, we ripped into ham, turkey, casseroles, pecan pie and every other dreamy food you could imagine. Then the time came to open gifts. As my cousin opened his, I realized that he was not getting nearly as much as we had gotten the night before. I began to realize that my grandmother had consistently short-changed him over the years. I knew it was wrong and, yet, participated in this type of activity for many years to come. I was just a kid. The revelations of the Christmas season seem endless in retrospect.

    The New Year brought many new struggles. I was still getting picked on at school. It was as if Daniel and Dontell just picked up right were they left off before Christmas break. At church, Brother Donnie's wife started to get him in trouble. She was not seen at church for considerable periods of time and, when she did come, she acted erratically and strangely. I heard murmurs of mental illness. Such struggles, however, didn't stop Brother Donnie from continuing the tradition of bringing lightening, thunder, fire, hell and brimstone down from the sky in church. Each week it felt like I was getting emotionally, logically and linguistically lambasted and abused. Once again, I began to experience terrors by night and day. Things got worse based on two events, a concert and a talk by a Christian singer.

Most evangelicals my age are familiar with the name Carman. He probably was the most lively and intense Christian recording artist of our generation. With cleverly entitled songs like "Witches Invitation," "Addicted to Jesus," "Satan...Bite the Dust," "The Courtroom" and "R.I.O.T. (Righteous Invasion of Truth)," Carman scared the shit out of upwards of millions of people. In the spring of 1995, I went to my first Carman concert at the Omni in Atlanta. For about two to two and a half hours, brilliant light shows, videos, pyrotechnics, singing, rapping and sound effects filled the arena with colorful declarations that the devil was slaughtered and Jesus was king. I can remember numerous stage actors who acted out all of these parts, including Jesus' win over a slimy horrific-looking devil as Carman sang. Through the encouragement of our leaders, we all raised our fists and chanted "JESUS! JESUS!

JESUS! JESUS!" in unison. I always thought that if someone of another faith had seen us they would have thought we were planning to invade Washington, D.C. and take over the federal government. It was pretty intense. Then came the invitation. "I want to know if any of you really know Jesus. Many of you think that you know Jesus, but have never really met him. Nobody can make the decision for you. The difference between heaven and hell is the 18 inches between your head and your heart. If you have doubts then let's nail them to the cross tonight. Hell is not going to be a fun place. You don't have to go and get burned up. Accept Jesus. He is yours." While he was speaking, all types of sound effects were booming over the loudspeakers, including snake sounds, lightening crashes, fire burning and others. After all of these exhortations, Carman demanded, "Do you know him? Will you accept Jesus tonight?" As the music softly played, he said, "Come! Come!" I prayed and accepted Jesus again. I felt like I was probably in that eighteen inches crowd who knew about God but rejected him in their heart. Then came the boom. "Many of you who prayed tonight are still holding out…mean it and give your whole life to God!" I didn't know if I meant it or had given my whole life to God. I was scared. Afterwards, the terrors grew more intense and I would have panic attacks late in the nights. My search for signs the rapture occurred daily and exhortations for my brother to sleep with me only increased nightly.

The preacher always talked about an age of accountability and I figured that I was getting close. "Maybe I should commit suicide, so that I could get to heaven, " I thought. The trouble was church leaders, perhaps wisely, never tell you the age of accountability. All options were on the table to truly know Jesus and get rid of all of the anxiety and pain. A few weeks later, things got even worse. One of the more popular Christians bands of the era came to our church. The band had been incredibly successful for about ten to fifteen years. The lead singer, Charlie, was giving his testimony in the youth group's Sunday school and my dad was the director. So, naturally, I got to go. Charlie got up and said that he had only been a Christian for about six months. This statement was shocking to us, because all of us had listened to his music for much longer than that. Charlie went on to say that he had always thought he was a Christian, but had never truly given his life to Christ. While on tour, he woke up late one night and was afraid that he had been left behind. I knew the feeling all to well. His response was to run down the stairs and turn the television to the Weather Channel. Thankfully, the station was still on and nothing had yet happened. Charlie said that he collapsed to his knees and begged God to save him. The response, he said, was swift and deafening, "Jesus spoke these words of comfort into my life...you are now saved...go in peace." I was terrified and my mind raced, "If this Christian singer was not a Christian, then there is no way that I am." Then, Charlie gave the invitation for us to pray with him and really accept Christ. I prayed harder than I had ever prayed before, "God please save me...please!?!?!" I began to softly cry. No relief came and I left the church knowing for sure that I had missed my last chance to get saved. Over the next few months, as Brother Donnie preached, I prayed over and over and over for salvation, "Please!?!?!?!?!" The pain and struggle only seemed to grow.

    In the midst of such strife, Daniel and Dontell continued to pick on me. Everyday, they would take my baseball cards, Goosebump books and anything else they could get their hands on. I was worried about God, sin, salvation and Satan internally everyday and lived in an external hell of bullying. I kept telling my teacher about it and she refused to do anything. One day, as I was taking my lunch tray up Dontell tripped me and I fell into my food in front of about three hundred or so kids. I cried and everyone called me a baby. About three weeks later, again in the cafeteria, when Daniel demanded my lunch money, I sternly refused. Chaos ensued. Daniel picked me up and slammed me onto the ground as all the kids cheered over the excitement. Then he started kicking and stomping my head. By the time he was pulled off of me, I was crying and bloodied. My teacher, who claimed to be a strict Christian, told my mom that Daniel said that I provoked him and that he would not be getting into any serious trouble. My mother's patience was beginning to wear quite thin. During the last month of school, everything came to a head. It was time for a bathroom break and, as all of the boys were in the restroom, Daniel and Dontell grabbed me. Taking their time, they hung me up by the back of my pants on a clothes hook. I couldn't get down and everybody else returned to class. I hung until my pants ripped and, after I got down, I went to the office to call my mom. I, too, had had enough. My mom came to the school and pulled Ms. Smith out of class. Our entire class heard it when my mom threatened Ms. Smith in the hallway with charges of criminal negligence and a legal suit citing intentional infliction of emotional distress. I heard the word bitch two or three times and everyone knew that my mom was serious. As the two boys who had been picking on me squirmed, I smiled and told them that they were next. The bullying stopped the day my mom got crazy at the schoolhouse. Two weeks later, I was picked as the most outstanding history student in the entire school. Knowing that I had struggled so much the entire year made it even sweeter, until I remembered that hell was always eighteen inches away from my heart. I struggled with my intelligence and thought that such an award might also be the path to hell. Though the external hell was gone, the internal hell remained. The next three years would rock any faith that I had left to the very core.

Newness

That which is new is often that which is old.

    My middle school looked enormous on my first visit. The walls were bricked and the windows were narrow. All of the kids looked huge. I was shocked to see people hugging, holding hands and kissing. In elementary school people just didn't do that sort of thing yet. At the middle school, there were even kids, who had obviously been held back, old enough to drive. On my first day, I was assigned to Ms. Donaldson's homeroom. She was a short spunky older lady who just happened to live close to my aforementioned friend Trey. When she called my name, I was scared. I didn't really know how to respond. "Here," I meekly said.

    The first few weeks were tough. I just didn't know that many people. But after a few weeks, I began to get in the groove. I realized we were at the point were it was cool to have a girlfriend. So, I sent a note to this redheaded girl in my class. Her name was Tiffany and she was absolutely beautiful. I wrote notes to her all of the time. Unfortunately, though we were "going out" for about two months, I never got the courage to actually speak to her.

When student council elections came about, my mom helped me to figure out a way to win the council seat of my homeroom. I showed up to class with tons of candy and refused to give one to anyone who wouldn't vote for me. When the results came back, the vote was 25 to 1. One girl in the class, named Jossey, said that I cheated because I wouldn't give her the candy she wanted. I guess you can't win them all. For science, I had a teacher named Mr. Pulverson. He taught us that humans developed from monkeys. I knew this was wrong and promptly told him I would not stand for his teaching such lies. I got my first detention.

I enjoyed not getting bullied everyday. I praised God every night that Daniel and Dontell were at another school across town. On most days, I was pretty distracted. Though I thought about God, the terrors subsided for a time. Like everyone else in the country, the O.J. Simpson Murder Trial transfixed me. My grandmother would pick us up and I would go home to watch the highlights of the day's proceedings. Unlike everyone in my family and at church, I was convinced that O.J. was innocent. I argued with everyone I could find about the case. At school, I found everyone pretty much divided along racial lines. All the white kids thought he was guilty and all the black kids thought he was innocent. On October 3, 1995 when the verdict came down, I was in Mrs. Lewis' social studies class. I sat on the edge of my seat and stared intently at the television. Then, I heard it, "We the jury in the above and entitled action find the defendant Orethal James Simpson...Not Guilty." I couldn't believe it. The class let out and I ran outside to jump and shout "Hallelujah! Hallelujah! Our time has come..." with all of the black kids. The white kids thought it very strange that I was so happy. When I got home, I told my grandmother that we had won and she said, "You sure as hell better not talk to your grandfather about this." I couldn't resist. When he got home I told him that justice was served and at this point he grabbed me and said, "A nigger got free today...Are you a nigger-lover?" I didn't say anything else. At church the next Sunday, Brother Donnie promised us, "O.J.'s day is coming my friends...God is not mocked...You reap what you sow...Jesus is going to catch up with him sooner or later...and when he does his dark behind is going to burn to a crisp." I wondered if he would have said the same things if O.J. had been white? I went home and asked as much at the Sunday dinner table. The response from both my mom and dad was swift, "Go to your room! You do not question God or the preacher like that." It seemed more often than not that these two entities were synonymous for them anyways.

Honestly, the relationship with Tiffany probably ended before it ever started. The closest we ever got to a conversation was at the annual fall sock hop. I asked her if she wanted to dance and, as we silently looked into each others' eyes, we danced the night away. She dumped me a few days later. I guess the sound of silence got to her too. It wasn't two weeks later that another girl was trying to catch my eye. Hamilton left notes in my locker and looked at me longingly. We started going out and calling each other on the telephone. The conversations of life and meaning were long and voluminous. The meaning of Coolio's "Gangster's Paradise" was a favorite topic. I also asked her, "Do you believe in God?" to which she replied, "Of course I believe in her and sometimes I think she might be black." When she said these words, I knew that I loved her. As was custom in the sixth grade, we broke up after about a month. I cried...but I knew it was inevitable. "Love is often fleeting" was one of my first teenage lessons.

At church, age-old friendships developed more quickly. The people whom I had known at church for most of my life became some of my best friends. On Wednesday nights, my parents made us go to a music class. The church's often-cantankerous music minister, Brother Wilson, headed this experience. In this class, I learned to be disrespectful and talk a ton. We broke up into groups each week and our group was humorously and pejoratively called, "The Rulers of Talkland." One night, everyone was making fun of the double name that my mother wanted people to call me, Jeffrey Kyle. One of the girls wrote Jeffrey-Cow on the board. I was chewing on a stick of gum and I knew right were I was going to place it, in her hair. I felt very good about myself for a second, until she ran to the bathroom screaming and crying. I learned from this experience that revenge is a dish best served cold. My mom forced me to go and apologize to the girl, Sharron. I had known her since my earliest memories, as we were actually only born a week apart. From this conversation, we quickly rekindled our friendship and probably became even better friends. Nevertheless, a few weeks later, I met Brother Wilson's cantankerous side. He was running late to the class and promptly handed out permission slips for our next trip when he arrived. Knowing I wasn't going to go, I ripped mine up and threw it away. This set off Brother Wilson and he snatched me up to march me outside. Grabbing me, with his finger popping back and forth in my face, he demanded, "Why did you do that?" I replied quickly, "I am not going." "Son you are a hellion, have you ever thought about your salvation?" he said angrily as he shook me back and forth. When he led me back in the room, embarrassed and defeated, I considered his question and knew that I thought about it everyday of my life.

Evangelicals have always been fascinated by the thought of Christ's return. My grandmother told us every time we visited her that the end of the world was quickly approaching. "You better get right with God, the hour is drawing nigh…" I heard it all too often. Brother Donnie only fanned the flames. Each week he laced each sermon with apocalyptic sayings like "…until Jesus comes back" or "…until that bright day when he comes riding in on the clouds." Through constant questions and study of the Book of Revelation, I realized for many of the people at our church they considered the book to be the fifth gospel. In the midst of all of this talk, I felt like Jesus was somehow lost. In the parking lot, I consistently saw the bumper stickers, "In case of rapture…you can have the car." The reminders of the impending end of the world made me feel like there was nothing to live for. I also felt a sense of urgency with people at school. In the mornings, students sat in the cafeteria from about 6:30am until homeroom at 8:15am. From about 6:30am until about 7:00am, there were only a few people in the cafeteria. Each morning, I went around and shared my faith. I told them that it was going to be really bad and that "the hour was drawing nigh." I went home and prayed every night that God would save me and keep me from getting left behind. I often softly cried, often until I just fell asleep, my pillow soaked with tears. I was terrified on most nights and days. Each new world event seemed to bring things closer. The assassination of Yitzhak Rabin signaled the rise of the anti-Christ and often my parents said it could be the good Southern Baptist in the White House, Bill Clinton. Fear was a commodity I knew well.

    When summer came, I continued to struggle. I thought God was involved and gave signs to guide every moment of my life. At the end of school, I broke up with my third and final girlfriend of the school year, a girl named Mitchell. The following weekend, I rode up to the family lake house with my grandparents. I realized I might have made the biggest mistake of my life when we turned a corner close to the lake and there was a street sign entitled, "Mitchell St." I knew that God was going to punish me for breaking up with Mitchell by taking my salvation. That night, I went to sleep at the lake and had a nightmare. I dreamed that I had been left behind, been forced to take the mark of the beast and been condemned to hell and damnation forever. I knew that God hated me and I had no chance. For the next few weeks, I fell back into deep crisis, depression and sleepless nights. I began to research my options.

I asked my mother, church teacher, and future youth minister what happened to people who committed suicide. They all replied similarly, "They go to hell...suicide is the only unpardonable sin because you don't have time to repent of it before you go to be judged by Jesus." I quickly took that option off of the table. Thankfully, one of the passages I read late one night was Matthew 7:7, "Ask, and it will be given to you; seek, and you will find; knock, and the door will be opened for you." I knew that my job was to ask, seek and knock. I figured I would keep pushing and God would eventually answer me. One of the bright spots of the summer was the Summer Olympics and Paralympics in my home of Atlanta. I loved it. My family went and saw baseball, basketball, volleyball, swimming and a few other sports. When Muhammad Ali lighted the Olympic torch, I cheered with the nation. When the bomb went off in Centennial Olympic Park, I cried. When Charles Barkly danced at the basketball game we attended, I danced too. Just like everyone else in Atlanta, I was convinced that Richard Jewell was guilty of the bombings. Later, when we found out that Eric Robert Rudolph set off the bomb to protest abortion and homosexuality, many people at our church thought that it was a justified use of force. While I was opposed to abortion and homosexuality like our church taught,

I questioned killing people to achieve the illegality of such practices. The games ended in darkness.

Although I had earlier in the summer asked about suicide for myself, the conversation became more real about a month to two months later. One of the more difficult moments I had ever seen the church go through arrived when a prominent woman at our church committed suicide. Almost immediately, the church changed teachings on suicide. We went from definitely hell and no possibility of forgiveness to Paul's exhortations of love and hope in the blink of an eye. At least for a time, Romans 8:38-39 overtook the Book of Revelation as the most popular sections of the Bible, "For I am convinced that neither death, nor life, nor angels, nor rulers, nor things present, nor things to come, nor powers, nor height, nor depth, nor anything else in all of creation, will be able to separate us from the love of God in Christ Jesus our Lord." I was amazed by the hypocrisy of it all, but found solace in the church's brief emphasis on the power of the love of God. We also found out that a minister at our church had affair with the woman that committed suicide when she was a teenager. I knew this stress wasn't her fault and I began to wonder if God's love might be powerful enough to save everyone. I didn't know, but briefly dreamed and wanted to hope. Surely not I thought, all of this stress and work has to be for some reason or purpose. The truth be known, I probably didn't want everyone to get saved, due primarily to the thought that it would minimize all that I had been through. I wanted our struggles to have purpose, meaning and consequence.

Darkness

Nothing is dark to you God.

    I made the football team. I practiced all summer for my big debut. To say that I was the smallest kid on the team would have been an understatement. I was the shortest and skinniest by wide margins. At practice, I got roughed up. I remember holding the blocking dummy and getting hit by the biggest kid on the team. I got knocked back at least fifteen yards and laid dazed until one of the coaches came and picked me up. I played flanker and was aware that I probably would rarely get to play. Though I played in two out of four games, I am still a little confused about what a flanker actually does. Lovingly, my dad always said it was similar to being a wide receiver. Regardless of the pain, it felt good to pick up on my dad's football legacy. It was nice to have something to connect with my dad over besides God and church.

    Speaking of church, I had waited for a long time to join the church youth group. I had always known the youth minister, Skip, to be the coolest guy on staff and was excited about growing in relationship with him. My dad had been his director of church school for a long time and I was quite familiar with all of the cool things that went on in the group. The Wednesday night service was called "LifeExplosion" and all of the cool kids were a part of the group. So, when the first night came, I was absolutely pumped. I had just acquired Michael Jordan's new cologne and I drown myself in it. I wanted to smell good. For some reason, my mom insisted on riding to church with the windows rolled down. I got a little ticked off about this, as I knew that she was airing out my scent. I protested to no avail.

  A few weeks later, we took our first youth trip to Camp Jackson. This trip was supposed to introduce all of us to the values and beliefs of the youth group and introduce us it did. The first night, I gathered with all of my friends whom I had known for many years. We were next to the camp's lake and decided to take out the paddleboats. Within a few minutes, we realized that we had committed an egregious sin when one of the leaders came running out and demanded that we stop. As we left, I thought that the incident was over. I was wrong. Skip, the guy who I looked up to so much, made us all pray for repentance and salvation based on this incident. Later, when he had me alone, Skip said he knew that I was the ringleader of the groups' misfortunes and demanded that I stop putting everyone else on the road to damnation. Such words were often used as a means for getting the younger kids in the youth group to behave. At nights, the lessons were consistently on the need for all to accept salvation. I prayed each night and had little hope that God heard me. There were two kids who weren't saved before they came and, by the time we left, they too made professions of faith. Skip made exhortations about heaven and hell being eighteen inches apart, the distance from your head and your heart, over and over again. I felt like each time he made these statements he was talking to me. There were also statements made that Jesus could come back before we opened our eyes the next morning. I went to sleep each night at this lonely cabin in the woods afraid that I would open my eyes the next morning and that I would be the only one left in the building. As I struggled to sleep, I figured out how I would get back out to the road, travel home and make our house into a fortress to survive at least for a little while. Throughout our trip, I remained terrified. For some unbeknownst reason, I was very happy to get back home.

    The next few months brought back the old exhortations of hell, damnation and tribulation from Brother Donnie. I guess the effects of the previous summer's suicide had worn off for most regular attendees at the church. During this time, two more major events rocked the church. A deacon and choir member named Jerry left his wife for a Latino woman. Though we had a Hispanic ministry at the church, it was separate from regular worship. I can remember seeing another deacon with my dad at the gas station and, after a contentious incident with the Sikh owner, hearing him red-faced scream at the gas pump to the top of his lungs, "Am I in the fucking United States of America?!?" The expanding and changing diversity of the area pushed our church. So, when Jerry left his wife for a Latino woman, everyone acted as if the apocalypse was unquestionably upon us. All of my teachers argued that divorce was wrong in any circumstance. The cruelty of this discussion was that many of the students in the class were products of broken marriages and homes.

    When we moved to the subject of interracial marriage things got interesting. There was one teacher of color in our class and she said, "Deuteronomy 22:9 is the primary verse of discernment in this discussion, 'Though shall not sow thy vineyard with diverse seeds: lest the fruit of thy seed which thou hast sow, and the fruit of thy vineyard, be defiled.'" Immediately after the reading, a young person of color visiting our church did the unthinkable and declared, "That is one of the most racist ignorant things I have ever heard. How do you know it is not just talking about fields, plants, and grapes?" The auxiliary teachers rushed to the teacher's aid, "Well that verse might not be the best reference, but interracial marriage is just not right based on the fact that biracial kids have such a tough time in our society." The young girl was not swayed, "Perhaps that is the society's fault." Though the girl sounded right, I didn't know what to believe.

A few months later, I found myself attracted to a black girl at school named Julia and was convinced that there was something wrong with me. I prayed for God to remove that yoke from my life. I felt that if my church or family ever found out, they would disown me. I set and stared at Julia while at school, convinced that something magic would happen and I wouldn't be attracted to her anymore. I couldn't take my eyes off of her. Over a series of months, I changed my mind. Though we never dated or went out, I fell in love with her.

The other major event at church came toward the end of one morning service, when a couple everyone knew to be going through marital problems went down the aisle. The husband reconciled himself to his wife and admitted the sinful nature of his sexual deviances. Based on previous gossip, everyone knew that he had some homosexual tendencies and everyone applauded wildly when he repented. I remember thinking that there was something wrong with what was going on. It seemed that the man's decisions were more a product of coercion than any new commitments. Still, based on what I had been taught, I knew that homosexuality was wrong and an abomination to God, so I refrained from asking any questions. It wasn't a few weeks after this incident, that I was questioning whether or not I was gay when I looked at some of the other boys' penises in the locker room after football practice. I stayed awake at night wondering if God was going to now condemn me to hell for such looks. The way that I was raised created extreme swings between comfort with the church's teachings, self-condemnation and self-loathing. I was always afraid that I was something horrible or something horrible was going to happening to me.

    At school and church, my friendships with girls began to grow more numerous. I felt like they offered solace and care that the rest of the world, at that time, could not. During Wednesday night services and on trips with our youth group, I stuck close to some older girls I had friendships with and they largely took me in and cared for me. At school, I became close friends with a group of girls my age. These groups contained disparate types of people that seldom got along. At church, the argument was always who was a better Christian. At school, the argument was always who was more attractive. The more these friendships grew, the more I was questioned at church. To many of the leaders at church, I seemed to be the victim of raging hormones. One of the main leaders forced me to never sit next to girls on the bus and said that I needed to hang out more with the boys. This was also the same leader who questioned me as to why I was sagging my pants. "To be cool I guess," I responded curiously. It was then that his response cut swiftly and deeply, "Did you know that practice originated from fags in prison who were trying to tell others that their hole was open for business? Is your hole open for business?" I was embarrassed, confused and offended by these and other condemnations.

    Throughout the previous year, sales of the first and second books in the *Left Behind Series* by Tim LaHaye and Jerry Jenkins exploded. Our pastor and ministers knew that engaging the end times keep people giving and highly engaged in what they had to say. So, in turn, few Wednesdays, Sundays or special trips concluded without scarring the shit out of you that the end of the world was ominously imminent and approaching. Everyone tried to convince people that the commercial success of the end times materials meant that Jesus liable to come in the next blinking of an eye. The Halloween season brought a difficult choice for me, to go or not to go to The Tribulation Trail. For people outside of the South, this phenomenon will probably seem unbelievable, but The Tribulation Trail was a horror trail based on the Book of Revelation at a local Baptist megachurch designed to get people saved by scaring the hell out of them. For all of us young evangelicals, we were convinced that what they were describing was true and unquestionably going to happen. We all tried to convince others too. I was really unsure about going to the thing. I knew that I had so many struggles with faith and the rapture already, that this was only bound to exacerbate my depression and anxieties. When I talked to older students at church, who had been the year prior, they said don't worry about being scared, it's just not that scary. My dad encouraged me to go and promised to go with me. So I went, the build-up to the experience was excruciating. When we were about to get on the bus, Skip, the youth minister, read aloud from the Book of Revelation. Everyone got real scared and I sat next to my dad. When we arrived, we had to wait in a long line. The Tribulation Trail was incredibly popular. Thousands of people, besides us, went through it that year. When it came time to get on the hayride that led you to the gates to begin your walkthrough of the trail, I got on back with my dad. We pulled up to a screen and projector. There, we watched a video that illustrated violent and evil scenes from all over the world, the entire video was serenaded by DC Talk's "I Wish We'd All Been Ready." If the images of bodies exploding and violence raging before your eyes weren't enough to terrify you, the lyrics that you heard in the background unquestionably were:

Ooh...

Life was filled with guns and war,

And all of us got trampled on the floor.

I wish we'd all been ready.

Children died, the days grew cold.

A piece of bread could buy a bag of gold.

I wish we'd all been ready.

And there's no time to change your mind

The son has come and you've been left behind.

A man and wife asleep in bed,

She hears a noise, turns her

Head he's gone.

I wish we'd all been ready.

Two men walking up a hill,

One disappears, one's left

Standing still.

I wish we'd all been ready.

And there's no time to change your mind

The son has come and you've been left behind

Ooh...

The father spoke, the demons died.

How could you have been so blind

And there's no time to change your mind
The son has come and you've been left behind.
And there's no time to change your mind
The son has come and you've been left behind

I hope we'll all be ready.
You've been left behind.
I hope we'll all be ready.
You've been left behind.
I hope we'll all be ready.
You've been left behind.

I memorized the words. It was my youth group's theme song for a number of years. If ever there were a need to show off for visiting parents our youth minister Skip's ability to get kids saved, this song would be blasted during the altar call. I was a ready accessory to such efforts and went down the aisle every time. This song was the cause of me getting saved hundreds of times. One of those times was right before the gates opened to start the Tribulation Trail.

    I wanted to make sure I was right with God before we ever began the trail. Who knows, God might come back before we were finished. The first scene was always the same, we were standing in a field, heard a loud noise, a flash of light and then people in our group disappeared. We knew then and there that we had been left behind. Though I knew it intellectually to be unreal, the feeling of God abandoning you was no illusion and I felt like I really had been left behind. My dad was still there and I figured he had been left behind too. I had very little ability to separate the trail from reality. We had been taught these things so many times that they all seemed so very real. Then, dark demons and monsters came up out of the ground and pulled at your legs. As you tried to shake them off, they pulled some persons all the way down to the ground. Our muddy clothes and red marks on our legs reminded us that the demons had almost taken us. Then you walked into an encampment that showed what people would be living like if they refused the mark of the beast after the rapture. As we walked up, we saw a family of five hunched over something. When they pulled back, we saw what looked to be the remnants of a young child. "We had nothing to eat and took the littlest one that we could find," they all said in unison with blood oozing out of their mouths. Then guns blazed and sirens went off as the armies of the anti-Christ and the New World Order raided the camp. They told us to come with them and we were run out of the encampment by people who looked to be holding real guns. The men and women kept pushing us and I was absolutely terrified. When blanks from a gun went off next to me, I winced urine in my pants. One girl in the group was crying and the officers of the New World Order demanded to know what was wrong with her. "You are now safely with the New World Order," he screamed and chuckled. Most of us knew from church that we were not being led to anywhere that was comforting. My dad laughed and thought the whole thing was funny. I felt like he was growing delusional from the stress of it all and didn't realize that we were only in the middle of the tribulation.

When we arrived at the next scene, a cityscape, we were forced to take the mark of the beast and someone came around stamping our hands with 666. A woman from one of the buildings shrieked out, "Abortions quick and easy…quick and easy…right here…step right up." The next building over had men with their shirts off rubbing all over each other. "What are you looking at? We are free to do whatever we want…" they laughingly mocked. Then the anti-Christ came out. Everyone in the production cheered. Some in our group booed and a woman that did, in hindsight obviously a part of the scene, was pulled out and asked, "Where is your mark of the beast?" "I am a follower of Jesus and will never take it…I never will accept or submit to any of these filthy acts…" she replied. "Then step right up…" they shouted as they pulled her to a guillotine. Shouts, guns and tanks revved up and fired off to the side to momentarily distract the attention of everyone. When we looked back, the woman appeared to be under the guillotine. My heart was pounding as the blade dropped and what looked like her head fell to the ground. As blood squirted out of her body, the anti-Christ stood to proclaim himself god over all mankind. "Who wants to be next?" he shrieked. Then the war to end all wars scene came, we saw tanks lined up ready to go fight the enemy, when all of a sudden the skies light up and Jesus comes back for the final time. After this scene we were ushered into a white room where Jesus sat on his white throne, a man who had died approached and said that he had been good to all peoples his whole life. Jesus harshly shouted, "This is not enough...you have never known me in your heart...depart from me for I never knew you." Demons came up out of the ground and pulled him to an orange hole. He screamed until his body disappeared. Then Jesus spoke to us, "Don't wait until you die or the rapture comes...accept me now and save yourselves from this fate...ask and it will be given to you, seek and you shall find, knock and the door will be open unto you...I love you and am waiting."

    A minister from the church then came out, "What you have witnessed is a dramatic reproduction of what we think is going to happen when Jesus comes back...there are signs all around that seem to point to the fact that such a return is imminent...or perhaps your bus or car could crash on the way home tonight...we just want you to be ready... Will you please accept Jesus tonight??? All you have to do is pray with me the sinner's prayer...volunteers will be coming around to pray with and record those who make a decision." When the pastor completed his address, he asked that every head be bowed and every eye closed, so that those who accepted Christ could raise their hand. As I raised my hand, for perhaps the thousandeth time in my life, I opened one eye to realize that most everyone else in the space, except for my dad, had his or her hands raised too. The certainty of my father extended to this moment too. I was still shaking as we got on the bus to go home.

Though I had prayed, I still had doubt that I believed in my heart. Skip, our youth minister, asked us to be quiet and for those of us who made decisions to ponder, "Do you really know that you know that you know that you meant it and truly accepted Jesus into your heart?" I was scared and squeezed my eyes shut to ask Jesus to grant me such certainty. When he didn't, I knew I was bound for hell. I knew that I didn't know that I know that I know that I was truly saved. I never experienced certainty the way that everyone else did. I had felt the God of love before, but I knew that such a being was a figment of my imagination. The real God was ready, unless we expressed deep certainty, to toss us into the fires of hell. I prayed the whole ride home and desperately wanted God to save me. When they turned on the lights of the bus for us to get off at the church, I just knew that that was the bright light, Jesus was back and I had been left behind. I timidly opened my eyes and realized everyone was still there. I got off of the bus and rode home with my dad. He exclaimed joyfully, "Wasn't that awesome?" Knowing nothing else to say, I carefully replied, "I guess so." His excitement about the whole thing or perhaps the darkness kept him from seeing the pain and terror in my eyes.

  The following Sunday at church I arrived unsure of why I was even there. The previous week I had stayed up every night desperate for God to save me and give me peace in the face of monumental fear and doubt. Late one night, my eyes wet with tears, I had begged God to give me a sign that he had saved me. I thought about the cross and, before I knew it, I was seeing crosses everywhere. I would even squint my eyes at lights to try to make crosses appear. This development proved to be new and lasted for the better part of two years. Attendance at the Wednesday night church service the following week yielded yet another discouraging surprise or development, Skip invited a man to give his testimony. This was not an uncommon practice. Many people had previously given testimonies about lonely roads, deep struggles, flashes of light, sexual struggles, audible strange voices and a host of other things, but this time was different. Instead of the person being someone from outside of our church, this was the son of one of our teachers and a deacon that we all knew and were very familiar with. We knew from his parent's desperate prayers that Nick had struggled for a long time with drug abuse and tremendous relational instability. His testimony, however, involved so much more. For those unaware, the time of testimony is considered a moment in which direct evidence of God's faithfulness, love and existence is given. We were taught to never question the veracity of what was said. When Nick began, close to two hundred teenagers were all ears, "I am a sinner recently saved by the grace of God." Although I was desperately unsure, I could stomach this statement. Then the terror began.

Nick started describing how in the midst of drug abuse demons started appearing to him and he saw witches in the trees. I was scared. Assuming we would be skeptical, Nick began to describe what he saw, "They laughed at me and said that God would never save me…they said 'Nick we are going to take you to hell with us'…I knew I wasn't saved and I began to pray…Jesus revealed himself to me and I felt a peace beyond anything I could ever imagine." I knew I had never felt the peace he was describing and things in my head were getting worse. I closed my eyes and tried not to hear what he was saying. Then, I began hearing echoes of the voices he was talking about saying similar things to me, "Jeff, we are going to take you to hell with us." Paranoia began to set in and I remained sure that I was going to see demons and witches when I got outside. I dedicated myself to not leaving. I didn't want to go. I knew the demons were waiting. Then, I began to think about getting left behind. It was all quickly and ravenously racing around in my head when someone put their hand on my shoulder. I slapped at the hand and just knew it was a demon. Everyone around me jumped and looked at me strangely. As I looked up I saw my mom speaking, "It's time for you to go to basketball practice." In those days, my recreation league basketball practice was planned for 8pm at night so that all the kids could go to church. I forced myself to get up and walk out of the room.

    The entire ride I looked to the trees and thought about the demons and witches that would appear at any moment. I was distraught and my mother couldn't figure out what was wrong with me. I looked for crosses and stared into the passing trees. The most ready location of the signs and symbols of assurance was also the place were the witches and demons came from in Nick's talk. I didn't know witch way to turn. I prayed and prayed until we arrived. I was scared to get out of the car and then ran inside. When I got into the gym, I was met by a ruckus. A white police officer was at the door mediating an escalating conflict between two families, one white and one black. A young white boy had accused the young black boy of stealing his Sony Walkman. The police officer rummaged through the black boy's things and found nothing. The white father screamed, "He is hiding it in his pants." The police officer, against the deep protests of the black boy's mother and our white basketball coach, took the young boy to the bathroom and strip-searched him. The officer, again, revealed that he found nothing and, turning to the white boy's father, said, "I'm sorry Frank, there is nothing more that I can do." The white father left with his family screaming, "Damn niggers!" As I struggled with the plethora of voices, events, and demons, both real and perceived, in my head, I started shooting free throws with my diverse team.

By the Christmas season, I had been in a period of deep depression, struggle, and mania for about two months. I was scared, seeing crosses everywhere, and trying to pray enough for God to hear me. Each time I had the slightest urge to sin, I knew that I was going to be sent to hell for sure. As the Advent season began, I walked up to the front of the church with my family to read the week's scripture and pray. Like many Christmas stories, ours was a lesson of expectancy, hope and arrival. Looking out into the crowd, I could feel their certainty in what we were saying, reading and praying. Such certainty, however, only made me feel the void of my doubts and fears greater in my own life. When Christmas Eve arrived, we planned to go to my grandparents house. It was the same struggle as the year before, the fight between selfishly wanting gifts and the realization that my cousin wasn't getting the same. During this Christmas, however, I dedicated myself to speaking up and asking why. The Christmas Eve service was largely a time of hope. Tom, the music minister, led the church in singing favorite Christmas carols and we were reminded of the porcelain baby representing hope for the world. Faith, for a brief moment, seemed simpler as I looked at the baby. Then, the pastor talked about the eternal price of rejecting the baby that was at our doorsteps. I became terrified once again and found it hard to even look at the baby up front. By the time we left, I was back at the same old depression and mania. That night, as we arrived at my grandparent's house, I asked my mom in front of my grandparents why we were not inviting the rest of the family. I was told to be quiet or the gifts would cease. As was usual custom with both faith and family, I tried to do what I was told.

    The New Year brought more revelations and struggles. One of the leaders who worked with our church's youth group,

Zach, was found making out with a fourteen-year-old behind the youth building. Some in the church made the determination with great anger that he did not need to be working with youth anymore. Ultimately, Skip relented and allowed him to stay around a bit longer after he promised to end the relationship. A few weeks later, it was revealed that the relationship had continued with the encouragement of the girl's mother and without the knowledge of the girl's father. As their marriage teetered on the brink of collapse, Skip made the determination that it probably wasn't a good idea for the young man to be working with the youth group anymore.

At the beginning of February, I got to go on my first youth ski trip. We headed up to Boone, North Carolina on a big charter bus. I was really excited, as I had never skied before. My dad came along and we all stayed at a crummy motel next to the highway. The teachings for the week revolved around standing up for Jesus in the midst of a dark and dying culture. The days were filled with skiing and fun. I remember this being a really sweet time with my dad, as he taught me how to ski. At night, we would gather in the crowded conference room at the church and worship together. The teachings were filled with illusions of the world's desire to pull us away from Jesus. The choice was Jesus or the world. The end of each night was always the same, a passionate altar call for everyone to choose

Jesus. In those times, I was often scared and hurting, I didn't know if I had chosen Jesus hard enough or enough times over the world. The uncertainty of the entire situation was almost more than I could stand, as I knew what the consequences were.

Later, during the middle of the week, one of the older students decided to show some of us guys the movie, *The Devil's Advocate*. About ten of us guys packed into a room to watch the movie together. I grew more and more afraid of the spiritual world, demons and devils, lurking all around me. Intense scenes of extreme sexual deviance, glass ripping flesh and other destructive activities made me cringe. Since I had so many doubts and uncertainties, I wondered if I might be the devil's advocate to the youth group. Such thoughts were unbelievably disturbing and I went to sleep begging God that he would rescue me from such a fate. Many of the images from that film lasted for many years after for me. On the last night of the trip, the group got together to hear of the cost of Jesus' death and the glory of his resurrection, although it seemed that we always spent far more time on the pain of the death than the promise of resurrection. Skip begged us to give our lives to Christ and said that he prayed that no one would be left on the side of this mountain in the event of the rapture. Such exhortations won me again and I desperately prayed for salvation. With everyone's eyes closed, I raised my hand as having had accepted Christ. I thought for sure that this would be the moment that God truly accepted me. Then came a time of testimony and, as everyone described all the horrible things they had done, I still wondered if I was saved. I thought about being left on the side of the mountain without any friends or family. I thought about God rejecting me. I opened my Bible to the 23rd Psalm and prayed, "Lord You are my shepherd and I shall not want. You make me lie down in green pastures; You lead me beside still waters. You restore my soul; You guide me in the paths of righteousness for Your name's sake. Even though I walk through the valley of the shadow of death, I fear no evil, for You are with me; Your rod and Your staff, they comfort me. You prepare a table before me in the presence of my enemies; You have anointed my head with oil; my cup overflows. Surely goodness and loving kindness will follow me all the days of my life, and I will dwell in the house of the Lord forever." I went to sleep thinking about being left on the side of the mountain. The next morning, on the way home, as everyone else laughed and giggled, I thought silently about that prayer and that set of verses. Though I was still terrified, such thoughts gave me hope.

  My mania and struggles got the best of me throughout the spring. The desperate search for signs of the cross pushed me often to lose touch with reality. I had many friends, but none seemed to remotely understand what I was dealing with. At school, I made As and Bs by showing up. Weird things started taking place at school. I observed a girl sitting next to me in one of my classes sticking her pencil up her skirt and zealously twirling it around. As she grinned at me, she pulled the pencil back out and licked it. This seemed too much like scenes I had seen in *The Devil's Advocate* and I didn't want to have anything to do with her. I knew she was possessed by something. My social studies teacher played Grateful Dead music often and I felt for sure that she was saturating our ears with music from hell. I began to zealously share my evangelical materials at school. New tracks that looked like money were just starting to come out and I put them in people's lockers all over the school. I joined the Fellowship of Christian Students in the fall and was zealously going to meetings as if my eternal salvation depended on it. I guess I thought that it did.

  The days were long. I got a new bully in the seventh grade. His name was Charlie and he was in my science class. Often, he would force my hand into a burner and kick my stool out from under me. When we sat at the desks in the front, he kicked me through the crack, no pun intended. One day, after he grabbed me and put me into a headlock, I had experienced enough. That night, I went home and told my parents what was going on. They sprung to action and made sure that they were in the principle's office the next morning. I was scared it was somehow going to get worse. My parents left after being assured that the meaner of the two assistant principles would take care of it. Mr. Hancock was no ordinary man. He walked with a limp, had a patch over one eye, carried a cane and was awkwardly heavyset. I am not sure that the man had ever had a good day. I sat outside and waited for the situation to be resolved. After three hours, one of the office aids walked by and asked if I was in trouble. "No, just pressing charges..." I replied. Unbeknownst to me, there was a camera in the room and Mr. Hancock listened to our whole conversation. I didn't think it too striking of a statement, but Mr. Hancock did. "Get in here now..." he bellowed, "We are trying to get you some help and all you can do is make jokes! I ought to send you out of here with no help at all! Get back in there, sit down and don't say another word until you are asked a question! Understand?" I and everyone else in the office heard him loud and clear. It was probably another hour before Charlie was called into the office. When he got there, I didn't have to do too much to prove that everything I had said previously was true, as he grabbed me and began to shake me as soon as he saw me. After he was given two weeks out-of-school suspension, I never had to worry about Charlie again. It was during this time that my friendship with Elisabeth began to grow. We talked on the phone everyday and I couldn't have asked for a better friend. I often would go home from school with her to listen to music and hang out. She wasn't my girlfriend, just my best friend. Elisabeth consistently encouraged me in my faith, pushed me to witness to people, and experienced all the same things that I did at church and school. Though we had similar experiences, Elisabeth always seemed to respond better to the pressures of church than I did. In some ways, I admired her for her fortitude. When she wore her "John 3:16" t-shirt to school, I knew that she had much more courage than I did.

  I began to more zealously share my faith, thanks at least in-part to the exhortations from Brother Donnie and training from Skip, and experienced some interesting incidents at school and after-school. Middle school physical education is always a madhouse. Everyone ran around screaming and the teachers had an exceedingly difficult time controlling us. One day, after we got in trouble for being too wild, we had to all go out in the hallway for about an hour. Although we were supposed to be quiet, I managed to make my way over to one of my friends and whisper softly. I had consistently been waiting for the opportunity to witness to Penny, a young Mormon girl. From Skip, I was educated to know that the Church of Jesus Christ of Latter Day Saints was a cult and in desperate need of deep spiritual cleansing and witnessing. Since Penny was my friend, I took the soft approach. I asked her if she wanted to talk about the differences between our faiths and she said, "Of course!" Little did I know, but Penny was taught to witness in the same way that I was.

Penny and I began talking and sharing. She told me that her faith believed that Jesus was intimately connected to our nation and had visited right after he rose from the dead. I was briefly taken aback. The church and my grandparents had consistently taught me that the United States was, at the very least, as important as many expressions of God. I thought that this had to be some kind of trick. So I persisted and eventually gave Penny a track showing what happened to you after you died. The track illustrates a man not paying attention to Jesus' call in life and then eventually being banished to hell forever. The track scared some of the hell out of me and I figured it would probably do the trick for Penny as well. Surprisingly, Penny handed the track back to me and said, "I believe all of that stuff about Jesus too." I was shocked. I thought that she was lying and I demanded, "aw' come on...tell the truth!" She laughed and said she wasn't lying. The next day, Penny brought a Book of Mormon to me and encouraged me to read it. I was surprised by some of its contents and asked her to tell me about a few stories. When I told a leader at church about the conversations, she encouraged me to get rid of the book before its demonic power overcame me.

A few weeks later, I was sitting in chorus one day when I began talking to Stephanie, the student who happened to be sitting next to me. I asked her what her religion was and she began to tell me what it meant to be a Jehovah's Witness. When she began to talk about idolatry and being against graven images, I thought that I could go along with that. I began to struggle, however, when she said that Christmas is a satanic creation. What can I say? I really liked the hopeful symbols and gifts of Christmas. Nevertheless, we kept talking and eventually we exchanged tracks. I threw Stephanie's track away and never read it, because I knew what my mom had said about Jehovah's Witnesses being crazy, annoying and evil. I guess I figured I was on the front lines of ministry and witnessing. We departed amicably and agreed to talk in class the next day. I arrived at class early and was very interested in what Stephanie would say. When she got there, she ran over, threw the track I gave her at me, and began to scream, "You are trying to corrupt me with filth and lies! You have defiled my family's house! Get away! Get away!" When the teacher got involved, I explained that I had just given her a track and that was it. Realizing that we had just religiously got crossed up, the teacher asked us not to talk to each other about our faith anymore. I agreed and figured I would just let her go to hell for acting the way that she did. A few days later, a girl in my class named Lindsey, who cut out pictures from fashion magazines, inscribed them to her self and told us that they were pictures of her family, approached me about my faith. I thought that she was very vulnerable and figured that she would get saved on the spot. I took the hard approach with her and spoke in much the same way that our youth minister Skip spoke, including hell, tribulation, pain, damnation and the possibility to avert all of that through accepting Jesus now. It wasn't ten minutes after I started talking that Lindsey knelt with me in the chorus room to accept Christ.

    Later that year, when Easter came, I felt differently about the sermon. Aware that he had been going through some troubles of his own, primarily with his wife's mental illness, I could hear Brother Donnie preaching to himself. In the resurrection of Jesus Christ, he found a reason to live love today and a reason to place hope in tomorrow. I felt like I saw the real Brother Donnie that day and I always viewed him a little more compassionately after that. As school slowly came to a close, I felt the warm summer sun approaching and grew really excited. I was particularly pumped about an end of school pool party that was going to be held at my friend Elisabeth's house. While I was excited for a number of reasons,

I knew, from talking to my friend about her next-door neighbor, that there was going to be a beautiful black girl named Shantee there. When we arrived at the house, Shantee was one of only a handful of black people there and the only black woman. I thought little of it until our youth minister Skip chastised her for showing too much skin in her bathing suit and for not acting appropriately. After forcing her to put on a t-shirt over her bathing suit, Skip spoke to all of us about the possible eternal ramifications of sexually explicit behavior. Then, without skipping a beat, he moved into discussion of the need to accept Christ and repent of our sins. Shantee, after some prodding, ended up praying the sinner's prayer and accepting Christ that day. I felt that something very wrong had occurred. I felt like Shantee was being unfairly singled out and pushed into a corner due to the fact that she was a black woman. I had seen much worse behavior from many of the white girls in our youth group. I remain deeply disturbed about what took place that day.

    The summer was a beautiful time for our family. Many of the previous crises of my life had calmed down, I settled into my questions and was truly happy for the first time in a considerable while. The need for the crosses didn't seem to be as imminent. We started moving into our new house. My parents had worked hard for many previous years to secure my great grandmother's house, finance it and get it built. They were really proud of the conclusion of their efforts and we were proud too. When July came, I was very excited about the youth group's beach trip. I had waited for a long time to be a part of what was promised to be a really fun time in the sun. My dad decided not to go and, in turn, I got to go on my first big trip of my life without my family. Freedom always feels refreshing. I boarded the bus, sat next to some good friends of mine, and rode down to Florida listening to popular Christian music.

I was really excited about our speaker for the week, Rob Maranke, who was the highly acclaimed author of *Satan's Salesman*. Everyone said that he was really funny and a tremendous man of God. The rules for the trip were laid out to us on arrival. No boys in girls' rooms. No secular music. No activity after lights out. No kissing. No drinking. No drugs. No pranks. No lusting/masturbating. The first few days were really fun and I loved hanging out with many of the older students. I found them to be much more exciting than many of the students closer to my age. On the third day, some of the girls convinced me that it would be a good idea for them to put make-up on me and dress me up like a girl. I thought it would be really funny and went with it. Everyone thought it was hilarious, except for Skip. He pulled me aside and asked me if I was struggling with my sexuality or if I liked boys. The threat of being considered other and cast out of the group was always present. The next night Rob Maranke began his teachings. For three days, Rob scared the hell out of us with stories from his days as a grandmaster or high priest in the world of witchcraft and satanic worship. On the first night, Rob tearfully admitted that, before he became a Christian, he sacrificed domestic animals and did terrible things to humans to please Satan and the rest of his legions of demons. On the second night, Rob talked about having conversations with the devil, through a talking cat, to do his bidding and his will. On the third night, Rob talked about beating the pulp out of the first evangelical Christian who tried to witness to him and how he participated in sexual orgies to please Satan. On the fourth and final night, Rob talked to us about how he was overtaken by a female demon who forced him into an affair, met an angel who spoke to him of his need for Christ and how he left the demon to become a Christian. The last night, as everyone cried, he asked us to accept Jesus as he had. "I am the angel asking you to come and know Jesus...don't be wooed by the devil like I was." Then, as tears flowed, Rob encouraged us to shriek out and wale to express our desire to get rid of our sins. It was a terribly frightening moment. I remember shaking with fear. When the altar opened, I and pretty much everyone else went down the aisle to express our desire to accept salvation and give our lives to Christ. Rob offered to us all communion as fellow believers in Christ. It was intended to be a climactic moment, yet, when we were told to make sure that we meant our decision for forgiveness before drinking our own wrath, I didn't feel much peace. I felt that I didn't know that I know that I know I was saved. The questions and doubts became overwhelming and began to get the best of any grip on reality I maintained. For the rest of the summer and into the start of school the next year, I went into a terror each time I saw a cat, worried that I was going to be attacked by Satanists, had panic attacks over my salvation late at night, was stuck in the juxtaposition of fulfilling the biblical command to witness to people and fearing I would get the pulp beat out of me, made my brother sleep with me, felt that any attraction I had to females was demonic, worried that some type of overwhelming demonic possession was about to lead me into a life of dedication and service to Satan and prayed desperately for help.

Growing

I don't know when I grew.

The eighth grade is a time of tremendous emotional, physical and spiritual growth. I knew it was going to be a big year. I decided not to play football earlier in the summer, long before school started. Many of my friends asked me why and I simply told them that I was tired of getting massacred to make them better. I actually watched the movie *Rudy* to try to find some encouragement to play. The movie only convinced me not to when I realized that Rudy spent years getting killed and bloodied in practice so that he could play in a game for a few minutes. This just didn't sound like a worthy use of my time. At the start of school, I began going out with a girl named Julia. She was one of the most beautiful girls in the whole school. I wanted to spend more time with her, but she always hung out at the skating rink. I didn't mind the skating rink, but my mom wisely said that the establishment was nothing but trouble. A few weeks into the school year, I found out a girl in my grade got pregnant at the skating rink. I figured my mom was right. The relationship with Julia slowly dissolved when she stopped answering my notes and phone calls. I just knew it was because I couldn't skate.

At school, I did well and found myself amongst the smartest kids in my classes. Most of my friends were pretty smart too and more often than not, evangelical Christians. Much of our free time was spent discussing God, hell, judgment, tribulation, sin and the eminent return of Jesus. These were still the days of the *Left Behind* novels and films. I actually had one friend named Mary who prided herself on being a regular biblical scholar. More often than not she scared the shit out of me. From the beginning of school, she prophesied that three deaths would take place to signal the coming of the rapture and great tribulation. When Chris Farley and Michael Kennedy died in short order, Mary argued that those were the first two necessary deaths needed. I prayed hard that night. I knew, based on Mary's intelligence and my own fears, the rapture had to be getting close. I prayed that God wouldn't leave me behind. Later, in the spring, when Tammy Wynette died, Mary boldly announced to our lunchroom table that this was the last death necessary for the return of Christ. I was terrified and knew that it was going to be any minute.

At church, Skip kept bringing in testimonials from the larger community. In early October, perhaps to prepare us for the coming Tribulation Trail or deciding that we needed to be rocked back into shape once more, Skip brought in a man named George who had just moved to our area from California. From the very beginning of his talk, George looked rumpled, odd, nervous and paranoid. As he began, "I have been possessed by demons and spoken with Satan himself," I grabbed hold of the bottom of my chair. George began to recount how he joined a cult of witches in California to have community and be a part of something. One day, while playing with a Ouija Board with some friends, George said that he began to convulse, shake and scream. Then he said that his eyes rolled back in his head. George started telling the witches that he was the great demon Legion and, with their help, he planned to conquer and destroy Christians. The bottom of my chair brought little solace. The group started sacrificing small animals to Satan, placing curses on churches, casting demons into other people and inviting unsuspecting Christians to join their gatherings. Finally, on a particularly heinous demon-filled night of wildness and debauchery, George talked about the devil arriving to speak to the group. After a quick pep talk, the witches and Satanists knew what they had to do, kill Christians. He said that cats and dogs began to shriek all over the neighborhood as this commandment was spoken. George said that he was conflicted and didn't know what to do next.

"Most of my family were Christians and I didn't want to kill them." The pull to do the devil's work, however, was strong. George quit his job and remained at home for many weeks wrestling with both God and the devil.

By this point, I was on the edge of my seat and looking for an opportunity to sprint out of the room. George then recounted how one day, after he prayed, the spirit of God came over him and subdued Satan and his demons. "Don't let the devil or his legions win or possess you next...I am a follower of Jesus Christ now and I want you to know Jesus too," he concluded. After his talk, I just knew that I was going to be the next possession. Our youth minister went up to place his arm around George and said, "I don't want this story to be your story...How many people want to prevent any more events like this and accept Jesus tonight?" As the altar opened up, I sprinted to the front with about two hundred or so other people. Everyone wanted to get saved that night. Not surprisingly, this was the beginning of a very dark time for me. A few weeks later, our church went back to the Tribulation Trail. Marilyn Manson was one of the hit musical artists of the time. The goth subculture was in full swing. I was truly scared of most of the kids in all black at school and I am pretty sure they knew it. Unbeknownst to me, my good friend Elisabeth took it upon herself to invite as many goth kids from school to the Tribulation Trail as she could. I didn't really want to go, but my dad pushed me to, arguing that he was sure that I would have as much fun as I did the year before. When I got on the bus, I saw about five of the goth kids from school and grew even more frightened of the coming experience. I just heard George's talk a few weeks prior and felt that some of the kids on the bus might be looking for a Christian to get their hands on.

As I sat down, I prepared for a long night. Upon arrival, I went through the line shaking and trying to make small talk, with anyone but the goths, to distract myself. The trail wasn't all that much different from the year before. It had the same terrifying effects and, throughout the trail, I found myself yearning to believe that God wasn't glorified through any of this. Toward the end, there was a scene that alluded to the Monica Lewinsky Scandal being a sign that Bill Clinton was the anti-Christ. I knew that time was drawing nigh and figured we might not make it off of the trail. When we came to the great white throne scene, everyone, including all of the goth kids, got saved. My friend Elisabeth proclaimed a great triumph for the Kingdom of God. When we got on the bus, Skip said the same things as the year before and pushed us to ponder where we were at with God. We knew that if we didn't produce fruit then we were never really saved in the first place. Though I tried to make it not come upon me again, life got scarier, nights were sleepless and God was distant. The more Skip talked about fruit, the 18 inches between the heart and head, witches, demons, the price of doubt, Bible reading and certainty the more troubled and frightened I got. I kept going to youth group and thinking about all of these things, because I felt that God, one of these days, was going to show up and fix me.

In the late fall and early spring, school was interesting for a number of reasons. I ended up having my birthday party in my grandparent's basement. My mom lovingly planned the whole thing. When my friends got there, we listened and danced to Hootie & the Blowfish. The next thing I know, my mom had everyone doing choreographed dance moves. She pushed everyone to get out there and shake his or her rump. I was really enjoying the party until my friends started coming up and complaining about the bossiness of my mother. Like many early adolescent teenagers would have, I overreacted. I began to get upset and told my mom that she had ruined my party. I knew these words would sting and I didn't care. About thirty minutes later, I regretted what I had said. I chose not to think about how stressed my mom was at work, how much she had planned for the party and other extenuating circumstances that made it a miracle that the party was even happening. I still regret hurting her feelings when she was trying to help.

Words can really sting. I wanted to help my mother...but I was unable to look past my pain and insecurity.

In early December, I received some horrible news at the grocery store. I ran into a mother whose son was an old friend of Newton Jackson and I. I was genuinely glad to see her and asked about her son, to which she replied, "He is doing ok considering everything with Newton." I, honestly, hadn't thought about Newton in some time and replied, "What is going on with Newton?" She looked at me dumbfounded and shocked that I hadn't heard, before exclaiming, "You haven't heard?!? I'm sorry to have to tell you this, but Newton is dead...He was struggling with his attraction to other boys and shot himself a few weeks ago." I was floored. One of my best childhood friends was dead and I didn't know anything about it. Brother Donnie's sermon the next week was on the dangers of the homosexual agenda. For some reason, I couldn't think about hell, sin and judgment, I was just devastated for my friend and his family. Christmas was a time of questions for me. I wondered about God's presence or absence, my salvation and what happened to Newton. I regretted mightily losing touch with him for a number of years.

The Christmas gift competition mattered very little that year. I prayed for God to grant me and all who were left some type of hope that would help us continue. By the spring, I somehow pulled out of the dumps and was enjoying life once again. Exhortations of hope being eternal, the love of God and the salvific power of seeking seemed to be real once more. Earlier that year, I was elected vice-president of the Fellowship of Christian Students (FCS). I kept all of my baggage hidden, so as not to disrupt anyone's faith. Each month, our president Jim and I alternated organizing a speaker, worship and conversation. In early January, Jim told me he would organize the whole event and not to worry about a thing. I got the surprise of my life when I arrived. Speaking to our group was the former youth leader at our church, Zach, who had been dismissed for making out with a young woman. I couldn't believe my eyes and was disgusted by his hypocrisy of the whole situation. "Give your lives to Christ and you will be amazed at the wonders that befall you," he exclaimed. I wondered what his definition of wonders included. Growing sick, I went out to the front of the school and cried. No one believed the story until it happened again and again.

Later in the spring, I tried out for the swim team. It was a dismal failure. I couldn't even swim the length of the pool and back. After tryouts, I went to the coach and asked if I could be the manager. He lovingly said yes. I dressed up in a suit every Friday night to help direct the meets. I really felt involved in something cool and meaningful. By March, it was

Jim's turn to organize the FCS event. I am not sure if he trusted me or not, but he kept secret the details of the event once more. When I arrived, the lights were out and Jim asked everyone to quietly sit down for the coming journey. The television in the room came on and loudly announced the film, *The Rapture*. It was a grainy depiction of the rapture full of terrifying images and scenes. No one in the movie can eat unless they agree to take the mark of the beast. The choice was simple, eternal hell or eating. The anti-Christ sounded soothing and spoke of the need for love and togetherness. Homosexuality and abortion made appearances in the film as representations of the darkness of the age. Then the movie got incredibly violent. At one point, a Roman Catholic priest is beheaded for refusing to take the mark of the beast. The final images of the film show the two main characters being killed for their refusal to deny their newfound love of Jesus. Then, without much hope of any kind, the film abruptly ends. All of my Christian friends in the room stood to clap heartily and express their approval. I didn't move. I didn't know how. The terror, doubt and depression overtook me once more. As I walked out of the room, I must have looked green, because people kept on asking me if I was ok. When my dad picked me up, I went over to my grandmother's house and stared absently at the sky. My heart pounded, sweat poured down my face, and life seemed hopeless once more. After I told my dad I wasn't feeling good, I went to the bathroom and tears flowed from my eyes as I begged God to save me from the misery of it all. Over the next few weeks, the choking darkness and hopelessness descended once again.

    In early April, a cute male swimmer told everyone I was gay and slapped me in the face. In that moment, I felt all of the rage, depression and struggles explode as I clinched my fist, aimed at his face and hit him back as hard as I possibly could. It looked like something from a prizefight when blood shot from his face into the pool. Immediately after, as all of my Christian friends chastised me for hitting him, I felt vindicated and somewhat proud of myself. I had finally stood up to a bully. When I got home, the swimmer's parents had already called requesting a meeting and my parents wanted to talk. I told them exactly what happened and spared no detail. After talking to me, I heard my mom call his dad to tell him that there would be no more discussion between them about the incident, they would talk to me further about my response and that he should talk to his son about the consequences of hitting people. Later, the swimmer's dad approached me at a swim meet to chastise me and tell me not to hit his son. I didn't say much. I was too worried about going to hell or getting left behind for saying how I really felt.

Toward the end of school, my parents, who had just started noticing my depression and melancholy, asked me what was going on. I broke down and told them that I had been worrying for years about going to hell and getting left behind. Lovingly, they claimed that they knew for sure that I was a Christian and that I didn't have anything to worry about. They recommended that I go talk to Skip. Late one afternoon, I went to the church and sat down in his office. I told him everything that was going on and how much I was struggling. His solution was quick and swift, "Have you ever felt bad in your spirit or heart when you are about to do something you aren't supposed to?" "Of course!" I replied. "Well that's the Holy Spirit guiding and interacting with your life...you don't have anything to worry about...just follow Jesus." When I left, I didn't know what to make of it all. I thought long and hard about what Skip had said. It seemed rather trite and unhelpful. The fears and terrors still roared within me.

The summer rushed upon me. Many of the terrors and fears subsided, for a brief time, as I enjoyed the many activities my mom always planned for us, hung out with friends, and spent time at both sets of grandparents' houses. It was during those lazy summer days, that I began to think about the meaning of my family's history. There was much to think about. My ancestors first bought the land that my immediate family and grandparents shared in the 1840s. I looked out at the field behind my house and knew that my family had been a part of the raging injustice of slavery and all of its succeeding evils. My great great-grandparents, about a hundred years prior, had built the house that we inhabited. The old fireplaces seemed to want to tell stories. My great great-grandfather's brother was a state senator at a time when people didn't get elected to office that weren't racist. In the parlor of our house, hung a portrait of my great great-grandfather. I often found myself scared of that ominous portrait. It looked like something off of a cartoon where the eyes appear to be watching you and then they start moving when you start moving. In the backyard, stood the remnants of a shack that housed the land's black caretaker for many years (who died in the early 1960s after living to be over a hundred years old). I found myself wondering what life was like for him. Up the hill, stood a gigantic red barn, built about a hundred and twenty years before. Occasionally visiting from the assisted-living facility was my ninety-six-year-old great-grandmother, in whose former house we lived. She told tremendous stories of days gone by and adapting to living in a modern world. As I ripped and romped through the fields and hills, I pondered and dreamed about yesterday and tomorrow.

In the midst of all of these times of pondering and dreaming, I was still going to church. I basically learned as much as I could about the God of love and hope while trying to tune everything else out. Brother Donnie was struggling mightily with the church's declining attendance and inability to attract growing numbers of minorities in the community. His sermons seemed to soften up and become more hopeful. Skip, however, was a different story. As the summer heat increased, his talks and sermons got hotter. I think he felt like this was the way to grow a diverse youth group. That summer, Skip had a series talking about the dangers of sexual sin. At this point in my life, I had been kept out of most sex education classes by my parents and knew very little about everything he was talking about...I learned quickly. When he told us that our penises would fall off if we masturbated, I was thankful for the word from God I got from my buddy..."That's not true...I know," he said. I realized that most everyone masturbated whether the church told them they could or not. This was totally new to me. I started thinking about some of the most hateful and damning people in our church being afflicted by their sexuality. I quietly chuckled at the thought that they had even remotely similar struggles to me.

Skip moved on to what was permissible and what was not. He argued that kissing from a distance was the only real thing that was permissible. I had never even done that. "I am so missing out," I concluded. Then he rattled off a list of things that Jesus hated before marriage, besides masturbation, including revealing clothing, innuendos, close hugs, heavy kissing, feeling each other up, hand jobs, touch jobs, lick jobs, oral sex, anal penetration and vaginal penetration. "Your bodies should not see the light of day before you are married...you can get pregnant from just about anything ladies," he concluded. After he made all of these statements, he passed around the celibacy (true love waits) cards for us to sign. "No one wants you to put your eternal salvation in jeopardy because they are horny," he further added. I got the message, sex was something to be afraid of, and quickly signed my card.

    That summer, I really got into wearing Tommy Hilfiger clothing. In fact, I got into it so much that I wanted to wear clothes that had Hilfiger symbols all over them. I rocked jean shorts with Hilfiger symbols on the back butt pockets (I think back and realize that jean shorts were never that cool). Skip approached me about my clothing and said, "trying to maintain coolness was a sure path to an eternity away from God." When the time for the beach trip came, like always, I considered not going. I knew that it would be the same old fear and damnation song and dance. After some convincing from friends and coaxing from my parents, I decided to go. On the ride down, as we passed some impoverished areas, I thought about the message of Jesus and wondered why we were riding on a massive charter bus to go to a place of fear when people on the outside were suffering. When we arrived, things, like always, got hot fairly quickly.

The first lesson was on the dangers of secular music and polluting our minds with popular culture. Toward the end of the lesson, Skip laid out the rules for the week and some additional instructions. A seemingly new addition, from the year before, was that we were expected to wake up each morning for individual bible study and a quiet time. I remember multiple nights of people staying up too late playing pranks and being unable to wake up the next morning. The punishment was always the same, extended kitchen duty. On this beach trip, we didn't have Brother Rob Maranke with us. This was not surprising, as many parents stumbled upon a series of articles describing the series of lies and exaggerations contained in his bestselling book, *The Satan Salesman*. Regardless, Skip had all the lessons and he did a good enough job of piercing our angst-ridden and downtrodden souls. Hell made an appearance each night and knowing Jesus beyond our fears was something that many of us could only dream of. Late one night, an older buddy came to me and asked, "Do you believe in all of this fear that he keeps throwing at us?" I grew sacred, as if I was talking about something forbidden, and replied, "I am just not sure that Jesus is as mean as they make him out to be." "Then, let's me and you be liberals," he quickly shot back. I wasn't there yet, the fear was still too strong, but I was growing.

    On the next to last night of the trip, one of the girls, Melinda, snuck out of her room. When one of the other girls woke up and reported her missing, we were all woken up to search for Melinda. From the way Skip was acting, everyone thought that it was inevitable that she had been murdered, kidnapped, or, even worse, been impregnated. After about an hour, Melinda came walking back from the beach with a couple of guys from another group and was royally degraded in front of those who were present. Skip called her mother in the middle of the night and reported that her daughter was sneaking out to cavort with guys. I have always wondered how her mother responded. The next day, before his lesson, Skip told everyone that it was a miracle that he wasn't sending Melinda home right away and then made her confess her sins to the entire group. She began to tearfully describe her initial contact with the two guys, sneaking out, frolicking on the beach, making out and deciding that she needed to come back. Skip asked if there was more. When she started talking about having her breasts felt on by one of the guys, I didn't know what to do. I felt like she was being intentionally embarrassed for no reason. I put my head between my legs and covered my ears.

The lesson for the night was on nailing our sins to the cross. Skip brought a large planked cross into the room. After he handed out small papers, we were encouraged to write down all of our sins and then come up to the cross to nail them away. Melinda was encouraged and allowed to go first. For the next half-hour, as the hammers hit the tops of the nails, Skip shouted for us to give them away to Jesus. I wrote on my piece of paper one word, fear. When we were finished, Skip asked us all if we had really given our sins away and encouraged us to shout, "YES!" Though I shouted, the fear was still present and the prior question only served to increase it.   Later that night, we went outside on the beach for a lighted baptismal ceremony. The kids who everybody knew were the worst behaved kids all got baptized. I even think that Melinda got baptized again. Later that night, our final one of the trip, all of the guys started playing pranks on the leaders. After about the third late night knock on Skip's door, he decided to tie our door shut. All of us were determined not to be outdone, so we went first to the windows and realized that Skip and the other leaders had screwed them shut. Everybody began to brainstorm and finally we decided that the only way out was through the roof. Though we ended up slashing the rope and getting out, I have always wondered what would have happened if the building had caught fire. I went home feeling pretty crummy about myself, God, and everything else.

Toward the end of the summer, Sara, a new girl at the church, who everyone knew to be gay, started coming to youth group and was completely ostracized. Skip roared against the dangers of homosexuality and I felt so sorry for her. Contrary to what was being preached, I knew that if Jesus was who the Bible claimed he was, he would have been her friend far quicker than he would have been all of the rest of our friends. I spoke to her on a number of occasions, but was genuinely scared of being ostracized along with her or being called gay myself. I regret not doing more. About a month-and-a-half after returning from the beach trip, in the midst of rising murmurs and complaints about Skip, a new education minister, Christian, arrived at the church. Brother Donnie thought that Christian would be the right person to lead a public forum for people to publicly lay out all of their complaints against Skip. When the night arrived, I was really unsure of what to expect. For years, Skip was such a powerful figure in my life that I thought he was untouchable. Then, the battle began. A contingency of parents spoke who didn't believe their kids were being properly ministered to and also questioned Skip's fear tactics. Shouts often broke out between those who were for Skip and those who were against him. I was torn and, despite his many scare tactics, I genuinely liked him as a person. I remembered the electrifying fears, but I also remembered the many times he had prayed with me and encouraged me. I felt like he meant well in a twisted sort of way. Regardless of my personal feelings, amidst the tears and raised voices, I realized that Skip was loosing support. This was the beginning of the end. Later, I realized that it was at this point that Skip started to raise up a contingent within the church to help him plant a non-denominational charismatic church in a whiter and more affluent suburb. Three months later, Skip resigned. For me, though it was the end of an era, it was by no means the conclusion of fear.

Dawn

I don't know what to do when the sun puts me in a daze.

Bubbles the Clown was arrested on abuse charges right before I started in high school. I couldn't help but recall the weird feelings I got when he watched my brother and I change clothes in the bathroom. I wondered how he was able to continue serving in different churches for all these years. Did no one think it odd that a middle-aged man kept dressing up as a clown for every single event involving children? Did anyone consider it weird that the guy in the clown outfit always wanted to monitor the children in the bathrooms? The director of the children's camp was next. Apprehended after masturbating in front of children in a parking lot, this was another man who had unlimited access to children. These events terrified me. With two church figures from my childhood arrested for child abuse, I knew that my childhood was over.

As I walked up to the school, I was scared. I was a midget in a land of full of giants. There were thousands of people everywhere. I knew about four of them. I felt alone and incredibly out of place. When people pointed, it made things worse. These were difficult days. I rode to school with my friend Zack. His family lived close to ours and his mom worked with my mom. For many years, Zack bullied me. When I was in a weakened position at school, he revved things up. Between the school and Zack, I finally got fed up. I broke down and begged my mom not to make me go back to the school or ride with Zack anymore. She told me that I was at the best school possible and that I was staying, but she agreed that I shouldn't have to deal with Zack anymore. This only made things worse. Now, Zack didn't have to answer to his mother for his actions.

For almost a hundred years, my great-grandmother was a hopeful dreamer who looked at the world as something to be admired, lived and adored. My earliest memories are filled with trips to her small house. A loud knock would bring her to the door, often leaning heavily on her cane. She always barked a joyful invitation, "Hurry up before I change my mind." The house always smelled old, but I loved the smell. The furniture creaked when you sat down and reminded you to be careful not to break anything. I loved the conversations. My great-grandmother was an encourager and pushed us to imagine our full potential. When something bad or good happened, she would often remark, "Everything happens for a reason." For many years she served as the queen of a residential care facility. The world was her oyster. The last time I saw her alive, at a hospice on the outskirts of town, I heard her cry out, "I am ready to go home!" About a month into my freshman year, she did. I still miss her.

Once Skip left, Brother Donnie started pushing even harder for wider diversity. The changes brought complaints about theft and misuse of resources also began to increase. I can remember hearing the innuendos. "They just don't understand our culture!" "Why should we even care about diversity?" "Are these folks even legal?" Slowly, such resistance began to break Brother Donnie down. In the midst of all of this, I began to realize that he might have had the power to scare the hell out of people, but he didn't have the power to preach the racism and prejudice out of them.

Brother Chuck took over the youth ministry on an interim basis. He was out of his league. Chuck's general lack of direction and inability to cope with what was going on led one of the church secretaries, Marianna, to largely take over the job. Marianna didn't have any children in the youth group, but did have nieces and nephews involved. Slowly, as numbers plummeted, from hundreds in Skip's day to teens in Chuck's tenure, the whole ministry began to orbit around Marianna's extended family. It seemed to me that Skip's enterprise of fear might just have been what had held the whole group together for the previous years. Deplorable acts began to take place based on Marianna's manipulation of Chuck. One of the teachers, that she didn't like, was the target of Marianna's niece's suggestions that he was gay. The teacher, who was an elderly man that had faithfully taught the class without incident for over fifty years, was promptly and embarrassingly removed. I didn't doubt that these actions were evil. It is interesting how in the absence of leadership, whatever leadership is left, good, bad or ugly, takes over.

    During football season at school, all of the Christians went to after-parties at the Jones' house. The Jones founded an international construction business a few years earlier and quickly became monumentally wealthy. One night, after a particularly joyous home football victory, I arrived to the Jones' cavernous looking house for a huge party. Before we were allowed to eat, we had to listen to Mr. Jones talk about Jesus. "Dedicate your lives to Jesus and you will never go hungry again." What would such a dedication look like? I wondered if it meant being wealthy. I oscillated between the desire to have the wealth that the Jones family had and the desire to truly be a Christian. A few weeks after the last party, I got word that the Jones called the police on a woman who came to their door and asked for food.

In November, I found my place at school. The basketball coach asked me to join the team as their manager. I started the following Friday night. I came to enjoy the bright lights and fierce competition. Basketball was a big deal in my town. I felt a part of something much bigger than myself, a team. Coach Jack was fiercely intense. During one of the first games I attended with the team, at halftime, Coach Corley flew into a rage and broke a bench over his knee. I thought he was the Incredible Hulk. I had never seen someone get that strong that quickly. In spite of the cussing, yelling, screaming, throwing and other bad behaviors, over the next few years, Coach Jack became a trusted mentor to me.

On the days that I didn't have practice or a game, grandaddy would pick me up from school in his stunning dudu brown and fire orange truck. I often felt embarrassed of that truck and, cowardly, I usually waited for him to pull way down the car line, where my friends couldn't see, before I would even get into the car. Each time, I felt really guilty about my feelings of embarrassment. I knew that my grandfather loved that truck, primarily, because it was his brother's last truck before he died. My grandfather was a troubled man who struggled mightily to cherish and hold on to the people and things that he loved. On those car rides home, the guilt was often drowned out by the long-winded lessons my grandfather tried to instill in me. Some were helpful and some were not. Nevertheless, I tried to listen.

Perhaps trying to follow in the footsteps of my grandaddy, I got involved in both of the business clubs at school. By the spring, I was a favorite of the advisors of both clubs and an accomplished participant in their regular competitions. I loved going to the conferences of both clubs. Each one had its own dances. At my first state gathering, a young attractive girl approached me, "You're just too cute... Would you like to dance?" I was hesitant, as I was not a good dancer. Before I knew it, she had me out on the floor. I put my arms out to take her hands as if we were about to waltz or something. "Oh no honey... Put your hands up..." she replied. As I stood there waving my hands in the air, she began to rub her butt on my crotch. I just knew I was having a religious experience. "Now grind at me..." she encouraged. I did whatever she told me to do. After some time, I began to feel particularly at ease, started to get weak in the knees, my eyes rolled back in my head and I felt something wet. I looked down and became mortified. I told the young lady that I had to run to the restroom. I felt so stupid for having peed all over myself. Young and dumb, it wasn't until later that I realized that it wasn't pee.

Later that weekend, I realized one of my teachers was gay. His passionate kissing behind the building gave it away. I didn't know what to do. The church had taught us to hate homosexuals and flee from them at first sight. The problem was that I knew I needed a ride home. I decided to give this one to Jesus and just not think about it.

A few months later, I stayed at school to wait for an open house. I walked by a classroom and saw everyone staring at the television. I knew something major had just happened. I rushed in and saw images of high school students jumping out of classrooms and parents frantically weeping. The camera panned over and I saw the name of the school, Columbine. Everyone in the room was stunned at the images. I told everyone that this must be a sign of Jesus' imminent return. I was in panic mode. I knew that Jesus was coming back and I didn't know for sure if I was in or out. My mother picked me up and she agreed that this was definitely a sign that Christ's return was imminent. My brother chimed in, "Mom you say that all the time..." Late that night, alone in my bed, I prayed that God would forgive me for booty dancing, not condemning my homosexual teacher, masturbating, not loving Jesus enough, not believing hard enough, not trusting the Holy Spirit and a whole host of unnamed awful sins. I wept. I prayed for Jesus to take me. The nights remained like this for the rest of the school year. The day before school let out for the summer, there was another high school shooting in the next county over. As the devastation got closer, the world seemed to be drawing nigh and my fears increased. Maybe the folks on the Tribulation Trail were right. God was ready to beat our ass.

I went to church because we had always gone to church and I knew my salvation depended on it. I just knew this was a sin too. My great-great grandparents were founding members of the church in 1889. We had a tremendous amount of history in the church. Of the founding families, there were three different sets left. Late in my freshman year, one dropped out and started going to a whiter church in the next county over. In October, when the time came for Tribulation Trail, the youth ministry promoted it as if no one had ever been. I knew better. I told my parents that I was not going this time. Thankfully, perhaps recognizing some of the previous trauma I experienced, they agreed that I didn't have to go.

The preaching at our church grew hotter and hotter. The youth group kept on talking about sex and improper sexual relationships. 'No this and no that' was the construction of most sermons. Brother Donnie preached that improper sexual interaction was a sure path to hell. Such exhortations didn't deter two of our church's deacons...who were both revealed to be having affairs. After the Lewinsky Controversy,

Brother Donnie moved back to a wider discussion of heaven and hell. I am not sure if he realized it or not, but people were beginning to be really turned off by the constant negativity. When people left the church, Brother Donnie began to argue that we were being persecuted for our beliefs. My parents, for a time, seemed to buy into his arguments. By the time the Columbine High School Massacre and nearby local school shooting had occurred, Brother Donnie was ready to unload. "Our time on this earth is drawing to a close and Christians better be ready," he infamously exhorted. Before he even had to say it, I was already there...

    The first year of high school ended eventfully. About a week before school got out, I was waiting in the cafeteria to pick up my lunch, when all of a sudden a racially charged brawl between ten different girls broke out right next to me. Wild mixtures of racial slurs and the word "bitch" filled the air, as I was quickly pushed to the floor. It was as if the entire fight took place on top of me. After I got kicked twice, once in the face and another in the back of the head, I curled up in a ball to withstand the remainder of the onslaught. I could see blood, spit and pieces of hair and weave falling all around me. The disgusting hot sweaty stomach of one girl landed on the back of my neck and slammed my face into the concrete floor. I prayed for help. Finally, after what seemed like an eternity, one of the coaches pulled me out by my ankles. Although I saw him speaking to me, I was too dazed and confused to answer. When I finally came to, I told him I was ok. I went to the bathroom. As I looked into the mirror, I realized that I had a big black eye. On the way home from school, I told my dad the black eye was from me falling down. Every tragedy was a sign. I started to wonder what it all meant.

On the very last day of school, I arrived excited about the coming summer break. I needed some rest. When the end of the day came, I walked outside with friends. As we waited on our rides outside, the most beautiful teacher in the whole school walked by. Whether we admitted to it or not, we were all in love with her. One of the crazier I knew looked at us and inquired, "Ya'll dare me to grab her butt?" I spoke up, "I think that's a bad idea." As he started walking towards her and reached out his hand, I screamed, "Watch out!" It was too late. The kid grabbed and squeezed. After letting out a yelp, the teacher turned around and slapped him across the face so hard that he spun around and collapsed. The kid was suspended for the next school year. I felt really guilty that I didn't do more to stop the assault.

During the summer, God slowly transformed me into something that I was in love with and not something I was terrified of. I began to realize that I didn't need the church to explain to me the abstractions of theology and life. I simply believed. I remember these weeks as a special time, due, primarily, to the fact that I haven't experienced but a few times like it since. I wasn't terrified of ideas or idealizations of God, Jesus, the scriptures and other manners of faith. Part of this had to do with my parents not forcing me to go on the annual beach trip. Life was good. I had many friends and we talked on the phone often. Freedom is an amazing deterrent to depression.

My friends kept encouraging me that it was time for my first kiss. I was in love with a girl from church named Sherry. After looking up her family's phone number in the church directory, I prayed for courage. Surprisingly, Sherry answered and agreed to go the movies with me. I sprayed extra cologne for the night. When I met her there, I was so excited. Throughout the movie, I held her hand. At one point, I leaned over to kiss her. Sherry looked at me and said, "You need to chew a stick of gum before you try that." Unable to find any gum, I asked someone in the row behind us. I found some. After a few chews, we kissed. By the way she said, "Thank you. Though I'm not interested in going out again, I really needed that." I knew this would be our last kiss. Still resting in the bliss of it all, I didn't care one bit. When they picked her up,

Sherry's parents cheerfully shouted out, "See you at church on Sunday!"

Consequence

The most real actions are the ones with consequence.

The smaller the church got...the more diverse it became. Brother Donnie seemed increasingly unsteady with the diversity in the room. Unsure of where to go next, the church looked for a sign. One morning something happened. As the sleepy organ music played, people began to clap along. This was not normal. The music minister instinctively allowed things to speed up a bit. After the song, people broke out into rhythmic amens and claps. Smiles broke out on people's faces and folks started swaying. Something supernatural seemed to arrive. Just when everyone thought it couldn't get any more spiritual, a respected older man named George stood up in the front row of the choir loft and began to convulse. The congregation cheered him on as he raised his hands, recklessly rocked and struggled to stay standing. "Get it George!" "The spirit just got a hold on him!" "Go! Go! Go!" Everyone was having a good time. When George collapsed, people assumed that he had simply been slain in the spirit. I knew differently when I saw my dad, the church's resident paramedic, race up and start performing CPR on him on the stage. Perhaps as a means of distraction from the wild events taking place on stage, people kept singing, clapping and swaying. Within a few minutes, after the nervous amens ceased, it was announced that George experienced a heart attack. Later that night at a meeting, the church chastised the music minister for letting the music get too swift and pushing George to have the attack. "Pastor, we need to keep things contained, when that spirit gets involved things get too out of control," declared the chairman of our deacon board. The church listened and seemingly banished the spirit for causing George's heart attack. Unfortunately, they also closed the door on many future opportunities for growth.

I thought a guy at school was cute. I didn't know what to do. All of my life, it was insinuated that such thoughts or feelings were reasons to commit suicide. While I thought about it, I clung to a belief that the love of God was enough to see me through. I pushed the feelings out and kept pushing to survive. All I wanted was to be able to breathe.

It was the fall of 1999. The fear was back. Brother Donnie reminded everyone that the end of the millennium was upon us and that Y2K was going to be the beginning of the apocalypse. Over and over, I prayed for God to not forget me as the world was exploding. Brother Donnie exhorted us to count down the days to judgment. At school, I would sneak off to the bathroom and kneel down to pray for my salvation. One of my Catholic friends, sensing that I was struggling, offered me a rosary and encouraged me to cross myself. I started crossing myself with the rosary each time I got scared. It was very comforting. I felt the peace of God. The very next Sunday, however, gave Brother Donnie the chance to shit on all the peace I was starting to feel. "Roman Catholics are demonic henchmen for the devil! The Pope is the anti-Christ! Each time that you see someone cross themselves...that is the Catholic saying death to all Protestants!" One of my friends, who had previously argued with me about crossing myself, started pointing at me during the service. It was as if I God singled me out right then and there from the pulpit. Well, if the truth is to be known, for all of us at the church there wasn't much difference between God and our pastor. After Christmas, the pressure reached a boiling point. I began to wonder about all I was going to miss. When New Year's Eve arrived, I worried so much that the world ending that I fell asleep. Around 1am, my father woke me up and carried me to bed.

For much of my childhood, God was a stranger. Though we were very religious, I was in the darkness. I had to believe there was more. There was. Close to a decade after the ending of this book, my life changed. For years I remained a fundamentalist, I was scared to believe anything else. Then it happened. The revelation that a dying mentor was gay transformed me. When the Queer God came over me like a flash of lightening, I finally got saved.